AF673118

Batukeshwar Dutt

Batukeshwar Dutt

Asha Kiran

Akashdeep Publications
New Delhi-110030

ISBN : **978-81-944528-2-9**

© Publisher

Publisher : **Akashdeep Publications**
1/1079-E, Mehrauli
New Delhi-110030

Price : 795.00

Edition : 2021

Type Set : Naissance Books

Printed at : Vishal Printers, New Delhi

Contents

Preface

Batukeshwar Dutt was an Indian revolutionary and a freedom fighter in the early 1900s. He is best known for having exploded a few bombs, along with Bhagat Singh, in the Central Legislative Assembly in New Delhi on 8 April 1929. After they were arrested, tried and imprisoned for life, he and Bhagat Singh initiated a historic hunger strike protesting against the abusive treatment of Indian political prisoners, and eventually secured some rights for them. He was a member of the Hindustan Socialist Republican Association.

The British Government introduced the Public Safety Bill & the Trade Dispute Bill in the Central Legislative Assembly. They gave more power to the British Government and the police against Indian revolutionaries and freedom fighters. The bills were defeated in the Assembly by one vote. However, they were enacted by an ordinance, claiming that the ordinance was in the best interest of the public.

After his release from prison Dutt contracted tuberculosis. He nonetheless participated in the Quit India Movement of Mahatma Gandhi and was again jailed for four years. He was lodged in Motihari Jail (in Champaran district of Bihar). After India gained independence, he married Anjali in November 1947. Independent India did not accord him any recognition, and he spent his remaining life in poverty away from the political limelight. The later life of the freedom fighter was painful and tragic. Being released from jail due to tuberculosis, he was not valued in independent India, he grappled with destitution. He was forced into starting a transport business for livelihood. Dutt outlived all his comrades and died on 20 July 1965 in the AIIMS hospital in Delhi after a long illness. He was cremated in Hussainiwala near Firozepur in Punjab where the bodies of his comrades Bhagat Singh, Rajguru and Sukhdev were also cremated many years before.

He was survived by his only daughter, Bharti Dutt Bagchi, in Patna where his house was situated in the Jakkanpur area. Dutt died in New Delhi, India from a long illness, aged 54.

This is a reference book. All the matter is just compiled and edited in nature, taken from the various sources which are in public domain.

The book is an attempt by this group of historians to understand the factors and forces that proved catalyst in the march of history in the subcontinent.

—Editor

1

Biography

Batukeshwar Dutt (1910–1965) was an Indian revolutionary and independence fighter in the early 1900s. He is best known for having exploded a few bombs, along with Bhagat Singh, in the Central Legislative Assembly in New Delhi on 8 April 1929. After they were arrested, tied and imprisoned for life, he and Bhagat Singh initiated a historic hunger strike protesting against the abusive treatment of Indian political prisoners, and eventually secured some rights for them. He was also a member of the Hindustan Socialist Republican Association.

Biography

Batukeshwar Dutt — also known as B. K. Dutt, Battu, and Mohan — was a son of Goshtha Bihari Dutt. He was born on 18 November 1910 in Oari village, Purba Bardhaman district, in what is now West Bengal. He graduated from P. P. N. High School in Cawnpore.

He was a close associate of freedom fighters such as Chandrashekhar Azad and Bhagat Singh, the latter of whom he met in Cawnpore in 1924. He learned about bomb-making while working for the Hindustan Socialist Republican Association (HSRA) there.

1929 Assembly bomb throwing incident

To subdue the rise of revolutionaries like Bhagat Singh, the British government decided to implement the Defence of India Act

1915, which gave the police a free hand. Influenced by a French anarchist who bombed the French Chamber of Deputies, Singh proposed to the HSRA his plan to explode a bomb inside the Central Legislative Assembly, which was agreed.

Initially it was decided that Dutt and Sukhdev would plant the bomb while Singh would travel to the USSR. However, later the plan was changed and Dutt was entrusted with planting it alongside Singh.

On 8 April 1929, Singh and Dutt threw two bombs inside the assembly rushing from Visitor's Gallery. The smoke from the bomb filled the Hall and they shouted slogans of "*Inquilab Zindabad!*" (Hindi-Urdu: "Long Live the Revolution!") and showered leaflets.

The leaflet claimed that the act was done to oppose the Trade Disputes and the Public Safety Bill being presented in the Central Assembly and the death of Lala Lajapath Rai.

Few sustained injuries in the explosion but there were no deaths; Singh and Dutt claimed that the act was intentional. Singh and Dutt were arrested, as planned.

The Tribune reported the incident as:

When Mr Patel from India got up to give his ruling on the Public Safety Bill, two bombs were thrown from a gallery near the seat of George Schuster. The whole House was dispersed in the panic caused. George Schuster and B. Dalal were injured while few other members received minor injuries. Bhagat Singh and Dutta were arrested by the British.

Ten minutes later the Assembly got reassembled. The Chamber was filled with smoke. Mr Patel adjourned the House till next Thursday. A red pamphlet "Hindustan Socialist Republican Army" signed by Bal Raj, Hony. Chief, was thrown into the blazing fire.

The police locked the Council House and prevented the movement of the visitors. J. Simon was also in the President's Gallery when the bomb fell. Sir G. Schuster, Sir B. Dalal, Mr Raghavendra Rao and Mr Shanker Rao were among the injured.

Butukeswara Datta from Bengal and Bhagat Singh from Punjab were arrested.

Trial

Along with Singh and Sukhdev, Dutt was tried in the Central Assembly Bomb Case, and was sentenced in 1929 to life imprisonment by the Sessions Judge of Delhi under Section 307 of the Indian Penal Code & Section 4 of the Explosive Substances Act.

He was deported to the Cellular Jail, Andaman and Nicobar Islands.

Last days

After his release from prison Dutt contracted tuberculosis. He nonetheless participated in the Quit India Movement of Mahatma Gandhi and was again jailed for four years.

He was lodged in Motihari Jail (in Champaran district of Bihar). After India gained independence, he married Anjali in November 1947.

Independent India did not accord him any recognition, and he spent his remaining life in poverty away from the political limelight. The later life of the freedom fighter was painful and tragic.

Being released from jail due to tuberculosis, he was not valued in independent India, he grappled with destitution. He was forced into starting a transport business for livelihood.

Dutt outlived all his comrades and died on 20 July 1965 in the AIIMS hospital in Delhi after a long illness. He was cremated in Hussainiwala near Firozepur in Punjab where the bodies of his comrades Bhagat Singh, Rajguru and Sukhdev were also cremated many years before.

He was survived by his only daughter, Bharti Dutt Bagchi, in Patna where his house was situated in the Jakkanpur area.

Recognition

The B.K. Dutt Colony in New Delhi, located on a prime location opposite Safdarjung Airport and adjacent to Jor Bagh, is named after

Dutt. It is the nearest private residential colony near to AIIMS in NDMC area.

Bhaswar Chatterjee played the role of Dutt in the movie *The Legend of Bhagat Singh*.

Anil Verma wrote a book titled *Batukeshwar Dutt: Bhagat Singh ke Sahyogi*, which was released on the centenary of Dutt's birth. The book was published by the Government of India's publication service, the National Book Trust. It is the first book published on Dutt in any language.

2

Batukeshwar Dutt : The Forgotten Indian Hero

Batukeshwar Dutt was an Indian revolutionary in the early 1900s. BK Dutt is best known for having bombed, along with Bhagat Singh, the Punjab Legislative in the Assembly on 8 April 1929. After his arrest, he and Singh were instrumental in initiating a hunger strike protesting against the rights and state of Indian political prisoners.Batukeshwar Dutt was also known as BK Dutta. He was a member of the Hindustan Socialist Republican Association, one of the first Marxist parties in India.

Batukeshwar Dutt was an Indian revolutionary and a freedom fighter in the early 1900s. He is best known for having exploded a few bombs, along with Bhagat Singh, in the Central Legislative Assembly in New Delhi on 8 April 1929. After they were arrested, tried and imprisoned for life, he and Bhagat Singh initiated a historic hunger strike protesting against the abusive treatment of Indian political prisoners, and eventually secured some rights for them. He was a member of the Hindustan Socialist Republican Association.

Batukeshwar Dutt, also known as B.K. Dutt, Battu and Mohan, son of Goshtha Bihari Dutt, was born on 18 November 1910 in the village Oari in Nani Bedwan district, and lived also in Khanda and Mausu in Burdwan district in Bengal. He graduated from P.P.N. High School in Kanpur. He was a close associate of freedom fighters

Chandrashekhar Azad and Bhagat Singh. He met Bhagat Singh in Kanpur in 1924. Working for the Hindustan Socialist Republican Association in Kanpur, he learned how to make bombs.

The British Government introduced the Public Safety Bill & the Trade Dispute Bill in the Central Legislative Assembly. They gave more power to the British Government and the police against Indian revolutionaries and freedom fighters.The bills were defeated in the Assembly by one vote. However, they were enacted by an ordinance, claiming that the ordinance was in the best interest of the public. To protest against this ordinance, the Hindustan Socialist Republican Association decided to explode a few bombs in the Central Legislative Assembly. Chandrashekhar Azad, the leader of that revolutionary movement, was not in favor of exploding bombs. However, others in the party persuaded Azad to accept Bhagat Singh's plan, and Azad selected Batukeshwar Dutt to accompany Bhagat Singh and throw the bombs in the Assembly.

On April 8, 1929, Bhagat Singh and Batukeshwar Dutt gained access to the visitors' gallery of the Assembly. At about 11 AM they raised the slogan "Inquilab Zindabad" [Long live the Revolution] and Batukeshwar Dutt threw two bombs onto the floor of certain areas of the Assembly which were vacant and not occupied by anyone.While the bombs were exploding, Bhagat Singh threw leaflets down where members of the Assembly were present. The leaflet included a statement that "It takes a loud sound to make the deaf hear." The bombs, as planned, did not kill or hurt anyone. This part of the plan, claimed by Bhagat Singh and Batukeshwar Dutt during their trial, was substantiated both by British forensic investigators, who confirmed that the bombs were not powerful enough to cause any injury or kill anyone, and by the fact that the bombs were thrown away from the people on the floor. Bhagat Singh and Batukeshwar Dutt quietly courted arrest after the incident. They were famously defended by M. Asaf Ali, but were both sentenced to Transportation for Life on June 12, 1929.by the day

Batukeshwar Dutt's Trial

Along with Bhagat Singh, Batukeshwar Dutt was tried in the

Central Assembly Bomb Case, and was sentenced in 1929 to life imprisonment by the Sessions Judge of Delhi under Section 307 of the Indian Penal Code & Section 4 of the Explosive Substances Act. He was deported to the Cellular Jail in Andaman which was infamously known as Kala Pani (Black Waters). He also faced trial in the Lahore Conspiracy Case but was found not guilty. He participated in the two historic hunger strikes in the Cellular Jail during May 1933 and July 1937.

BHAGAT SINGH AND BATUKESHWAR DUTT'S

Letter Addressed to Home Member , Government of India

Central Jail Lahore

24-6-1929

We , Bhagat Singh and BK. Dutt were sentenced to life transportation in the Assembly Bomb Case, Delhi, on the 19th April, 1929. As long as we were undertrial prisoners in Delhi Jail, we were accorded a very good treatment from that jail to the Mianwali and Lahore Central Jails respectively, we wrote an application to the higher authorities asking for better diet and a few other facilities, and refused to take the jail diet. Our demands were as follows:

1. We, as political prisoners, should be given better diet and the standard of our diet should at least be the same as that of European prisoners. (It is not the sameness of dietary that we demand, but the sameness of standard of diet.)
2. We shall no be forced to do any hard and undignified lobours at all.
3. All books, other than those proscribed, along with writing materials, should be allowed to us without any restriction.
4. At least one standard daily paper should be supplied to every political prisoner.
5. Political prisoners should have a special ward of their own in every jail, provided with all necessities as those of the europeans. And all the political prisoners in one jail must be kept together in that ward.

6. Toilet necessities should be supplied.
7. Better clothing.

We have explained above the demands that we made. They are the most reasonable demands. The Jail authorities told us one day that the higher authorities have refused to comply with our demands.

Apart from that, they handle us very roughly while feeding us artificially, and Bhagat Singh was lying quite senseless on the 10th June, 1929, for about 15 mts., after the forcible feeding, which we request to be stopped without any further delay.

In addition, we may be permitted to refer to the recommendations made in the U.P. Jail Committee by Pt. Jagat Narain and K.B. Hafiz Hidayat Hussain. They have recommended the political prisoners to be treated as "Better Class Prisoners." We request you to kindly consider our demands at your earliest convenience.

- By "Political Prisoners", we mean all those people who are convicted for offences against the State, for instane the people who were convicted in the Lahore Conspiracy Cases, 1915-17, the Kakori Conspiracy Cases and Sedition Cases in general.

Yours

Bhagat Singh

B.K. Dutt

Last Days of Batukeshwar Dutt

After his release from prison Batukeshwar Dutt contracted tuberculosis. He nonetheless participated in the Quit India Movement of Mahatma Gandhi and was again jailed for four years.

After India gained independence, he married Anjali in November 1947. It is sad that independent India did not accord him any recognition, and he spent his remaining life in penury away from political limelight, a forgotten hero. Batukeshwar Dutt outlived all his comrades and died on 20 July 1965 in the AIIMS in Delhi after his long illness. He was cremated in Hussainiwala near Firozepur in Punjab where the bodies of his comrades Bhagat Singh, Rajguru and Sukhdev were also cremated many years ago. He was survived by his only daughter, Mrs. Bharti Bagchi, in Patna where his house was situated in the Jakkanpur area.

The B.K. Dutt Colony in New Delhi is named after Batukeshwar Dutt death.

BATUKESHWAR DUTT: INTERESTING FACTS ABOUT THE FORGOTTEN HERO

Batukeshwar Dutt or BK Dutt was born on this day, November 18, in the year 1910. He was a close associate of Bhagat Singh and was his accomplice in various movements.

Listed below are some lesser-known facts about the revolutionary:

- While Working for the Hindustan Socialist Republican Association in Kanpur, Dutt learned how to make bombs
- He was a close associate of freedom fighters Chandrashekhar Azad and Bhagat Singh
- He exploded bombs along with Bhagat Singh, in the Central Legislative Assembly in New Delhi on April 8, 1929
- After they were arrested, tried and imprisoned for life, they were deported to the Cellular Jail (Kaala Paani) in Andaman
- While serving the term, Dutt initiated a historic hunger strike along with Bhagat Singh to protest against the abusive treatment of Indian political prisoners, and eventually secured some rights for them
- After his release from prison, he contracted tuberculosis (TB); however, that did not deter him from participating in the Quit India Movement. The act landed him in jail for another four years
- He died on January 20, 1965 in AIIMS hospital after battling illness for a long time.

3

Batukeshwar Dutta and Hindustan Socialist Republican Association

BATUKESHWAR DUTT: ONE OF THE UNSUNG HEROES OF THE YOUNG HINDU REVOLUTIONARIES

Best known for having exploded a few bombs along with Bhagat Singh in the Central Legislative Assembly in New Delhi on April 8, 1929, Batukeshwar Dutt was an Indian revolutionary and a freedom fighter in the early 1900s.

After they were arrested, tried and imprisoned for life, he and Bhagat Singh initiated a historic hunger strike protesting against the abusive treatment of Indian political prisoners, and eventually secured some rights for them. Batukeshwar was a member of the Hindustan Socialist Republican Association.

Early life

Batukeshwar Dutt, born on November 18, 1910 in Oari village, Burdwan district, in what is now West Bengal, was a son of Goshtha Bihari Dutt. He graduated from PPN high school in Kanpur, and was also known as BK Dutt, Battu, and Mohan. He was a close associate of freedom fighters such as Chandrashekhar Azad and Bhagat Singh; he met the latter in Kanpur in 1924, where he learned about bomb-making while working for the Hindustan Socialist Republican Association (HSRA).

Bombs in the Assembly

The British Government introduced the Public Safety Bill and the Trade Dispute Bill in the Central Legislative Assembly. They gave more power to the British Government and the police against Indian revolutionaries and freedom fighters. The bills were defeated in the Assembly by one vote. However, they were enacted by an ordinance, claiming that the ordinance was in the best interest of the public. To protest against this ordinance, the Hindustan Socialist Republican Association decided to explode a few bombs in the Central Legislative Assembly. Chandrashekhar Azad, the leader of that revolutionary movement, was not in favour of exploding bombs. However, others in the party persuaded Azad to accept Bhagat Singh's plan, and Azad selected Batukeshwar Dutt to accompany Bhagat Singh and throw the bombs in the Assembly.

Trial

Along with his comrades Bhagat Singh and Sukhdev Thapar, Batukeshwar Dutt was tried in the Central Assembly Bomb Case, and was sentenced in 1929 to life imprisonment by the Sessions Judge of Delhi under Section 307 of the Indian Penal Code and Section 4 of the Explosive Substances Act. He was deported to the Cellular Jail, Andaman and Nicobar Islands.

Last days

Batukeshwar Dutt was repatriated to the mainland in 1937, and was later released from the Bankipur Jail in Patna in 1938. After his release from prison, he contracted tuberculosis. He nonetheless participated in the Quit India Movement of Mahatma Gandhi and was again jailed for four years. He was lodged in Motihari Jail (in Champaran district of Bihar). After India gained independence, he married Anjali in November 1947. Independent India did not accord him any recognition, and he spent the rest of his life in poverty away from the political limelight. Batukeshwar Dutt outlived all his comrades and died on 20 July 1965 in AIIMS in Delhi after a long illness. He was cremated in Hussainiwala near Firozepur in Punjab where the bodies of his comrades Bhagat Singh, Rajguru and Sukhdev were also cremated many years before. He was survived by his only daughter, Mrs Bharti Bagchi, in Patna where his house was situated in the Jakkanpur area.

Colony in Delhi

The BK Dutt Colony in New Delhi, located in a prime location opposite Safdarjung Airport and adjacent to Jor Bagh, is named after Batukeshwar Dutt. This is the nearest private residential colony to AIIMS in the area.

Film

Bhaswar Chatterjee played the role of BK Dutt in the movie *The Legend of Bhagat Singh*, directed by Rajkumar Santoshi. Released on June 7, 2002, the movie won two National Film Awards, including the National Film Award for Best Feature Film in Hindi, and three Filmfare Awards, including the Filmfare Critics Award for Best Movie.

Book

Anil Verma wrote a book titled *Batukeshwar Dutt: Bhagat Singh ke Sahyogi*, which was released on the centenary of Dutt's birth on November 18. The book was published by the Government of India's publication service, the National Book Trust. It is the first book published on Batukeshwar Dutt in any language.

H.R.A. AND THE KAKORI CONSPIRACY CASE

It was in the background of all these historic events that Bhagat Singh reached Kanpur in 1924. There he went to his father's friend Ganesh Shankar Vidyarthi, a prominent Congress leader and the editor of Pratap. Though Vidyarthi was himself a Gandhian, his house was a common meeting place for socialists, communists and other revolutionaries. It was here that Bhagat Singh met Chandrashekhar Azad, Batukeshwar Dutt, Jogesh Chandra Chatterjee,

Shiv Verma, Bejoy Kumar Sinha and others. In Kanpur, he continued to read voraciously and completed his study of Karl Marx's Capital. He wrote and distributed nationalist and revolutionary leaflets amongst the masses. It was in his six months stay at Kanpur that he joined the Hindustan Republican Association (HRA).

The HRA had been formed in 1923-within a year of Chauri Chaura and its aftermath-by Sachindranath Sanyal, who was transported for life in the Banaras Conspiracy Case and later released. He was a close associate of Rash Behari Bose. Sanyal's book written in jail, Bandi Jeevan, was highly acclaimed by all armed freedom fighters of that era. Sanyal had written the Manifesto of the HRA, which was distributed in all major cities of North India on the night between December 31, 1924 and January 1, 1925. He had also prepared the HRA Constitution, which came to be known as the Yellow Paper. The HRA Manifesto, which was titled The Revolutionary, was a powerful piece that began thus, "Chaos is necessary to the birth of a new star. And the birth of life is accompanied by agony and pain. India is also taking a new birth, and is passing through that inevitable chaos and agony. Indians shall play their destined role, when all calculations shall prove futile, when the wise and the mighty shall be bewildered by the simple and the weak, when great empires shall crumble down and new nations shall arise and surprise humanity with the splendour and glory which shall be all its own."

It then set out its aim: "The immediate object of the revolutionary party in the domain of politics is to establish a federal Republic of United States of India by an organized and armed revolution. The final constitution of this Republic shall be framed and declared at a time when the representatives of India shall have the power to carry out their decision. But the basic principles of this Republic will be universal suffrage and abolition of all systems which make the exploitation of man by man possible, e.g. the railways and other means of transportation and communication, the mines and other kinds of very great industries such as the manufacture of steel and ships, all these shall be nationalized."

Further, "The revolutionary party is not national but international in the sense that its ultimate object is to bring harmony in the world by respecting and guaranteeing the diverse interests of the different nations. It aims not at competition but at cooperation between the different nations and states and in this respect it follows the footsteps of the great Indian rishis of the glorious past and of Bolshevik Russia in the modern age."

The HRA Manifesto and Constitution had their strengths and their weaknesses, which were neatly summarized by Satyendra Narayan Mazumdar in his book In Search of A Revolutionary Ideology and A Revolutionary Programme as follows, "The above two documents may be described as typical of the thinking of those revolutionaries who were then being attracted towards communism, yet could not completely overcome the influence of romantic revolutionism." While showing a positive but confused inclination towards socialism, the Manifesto also had marked elements of mysticism.

Funds for procuring arms and ammunition were raised by the HRA, among other methods, by committing dacoities. Some minor dacoities went unnoticed. But on August 9, 1925, the HRA revolutionaries stopped a train at Kakori near Lucknow and broke a government safe carrying a modest amount of Rs 4679.

Despite warning the train passengers not to come out so that no harm would come to them, one person came out and was accidentally killed. The British government cracked down brutally, instituted the Kakori Conspiracy Case and managed to arrest most of the participants in the dacoity. Ram Prasad Bismil, Ashfaqullah Khan and Thakur Roshan Singh were hanged on December 19, 1927 and Rajendra Lahiri two days earlier on December 17, 1927. Sachindranath Sanyal and Jogesh Chandra Chatterjee got life imprisonment, while 11 others got various terms in jail. Only Chandrashekhar Azad and Kundan Lal Gupta escaped arrest. This was a big blow to the HRA, but it recovered due to the great efforts of Chandrashekhar Azad and the second line of leadership comprising Shiv Verma and others.

The Kakori martyrs became a legend throughout India. On the day of his execution, Ram Prasad Bismil declared, "We shall be born again, shall meet again and shall jointly fight once again for the cause of the motherland as comrades-in-arms." Ashfaqullah Khan told his nephew the day before his execution, "You must remember that the Hindu community has dedicated and great souls like Khudiram and Kanailal. To me, this is my good fortune that, belonging to the Muslim community, I have acquired the privilege of following in the footsteps of those great martyrs." The death-defying song they sang to the gallows became part of the lexicon of the freedom struggle. This song was:

Sarfaroshi ki tamanna ab hamare dil mein hai,

Dekhna hai zor kitna baju-e katil mein hai.

(We have now a longing in our hearts to put our heads on to the bidding,

It is to be seen how much strength the executioner has in his arms.)

NAUJAWAN BHARAT SABHA

Before the Kakori dacoity, in early 1925, Bhagat Singh had gone back to Lahore when his father assured him that he would not be married off against his wishes. He started political work and set up the Lahore branch of the HRA, but had to shift to Delhi for six months in 1925 to evade arrest. In Delhi, he worked with the daily Veer Arjun. In late 1925, he went to Kanpur to take part in abortive attempts to free the Kakori prisoners from jail and soon returned to Lahore.

Here, Bhagat Singh along with Bhagwati Charan Vohra, Sukhdev and Ram Krishan took the lead in forming a militant youth organization called the Naujawan Bharat Sabha (NBS) in March 1926. Ram Krishan was elected its president and Bhagat Singh its secretary. Its members also included eminent personalities like Saifuddin Kitchlew, Satyapal, Mir Abdul Majid, Sardul Singh Caveeshar and the poet Lal Chand Falak.

The founding of the NBS as an open wing of the revolutionaries to carry out political work among the youth, peasants and workers was a very significant step in the political and ideological journey of Bhagat Singh. It showed his growing Marxist conviction that popular broad-based mass movements alone could lead to a successful revolution. This mass approach is reflected in the Aims and Manifesto of the NBS, partly quoted below.

The NBS soon opened branches at Lahore, Amritsar and other cities and towns in Punjab and, later, at Karachi and Peshawar as well. Bhagat Singh and his colleagues delivered inspiring lectures on the lives of revolutionary martyrs in NBS meetings, the aim being to rouse the youth against British imperialism. In June 1928, Bhagat Singh and Sukhdev also organized the Lahore Students' Union, as an auxiliary of the NBS. Both organizations served as a recruiting ground for the HSRA which was to be formed later. In August 1928, the NBS, along with radical Congressmen, celebrated "Friends of Russia Week" and also organized a meeting to eulogize the Russian Revolution. From 1928-30, HSRA revolutionaries and Communist groups worked together in the NBS. The NBS was banned by the British government in May 1930, a year after Bhagat Singh's arrest.

The political aims of the NBS were: (a) To establish a completely independent republic of the labourers and peasants of the whole of India, (b) To infuse a spirit of patriotism in the hearts of the youth of the country in order to establish a united Indian nation, (c) To express sympathy with and to assist economic, industrial and social movements, which, being free from communal sentiments, were intended to take the movement nearer its ideal, d) To organize labourers and peasants.

The Manifesto of the NBS, written by Bhagwati Charan Vohra on April 6, 1928, declared: "The future programme of preparing the country will begin with the motto: 'Revolution by the masses and for the masses.' In other words, Swaraj for the 90%; Swaraj not only attained by the masses but also for the masses...Without going into details, we can safely assert that to achieve our object, thousands of our most brilliant young men, like Russian youth, will have to pass their precious lives in villages and make the people understand what the Indian revolution would really mean. They must be made to realize that the revolution which is to come will mean more than a change of masters. It will, above all, mean the birth of a new order of things, a new state. This is not the work of a day or a year. Decades of matchless self-sacrifice will prepare the masses for the accomplishment of that great work and only the revolutionary young men will be able to do that. A revolutionary does not necessarily mean a man of bombs and revolvers."

Outlining the close links between the NBS and the Communists, A.G. Noorani writes in The Trial of Bhagat Singh: Politics of Justice: "The Sabha's progress was impressive by any standards. Similar bodies were formed in other provinces. Branches proliferated in the Punjab. An All-India Naujawan Bharat Sabha was established in Delhi. Soon links were forged with the Hindustan Republican Association and the Kirti Kisan Party, founded by Sohan Singh Josh.

Already, on his return to Lahore, Bhagat Singh had established contacts with the Kirti Kisan Party. The Party owed its existence to the united efforts of the emissaries of the Ghadar Party (Bhag Singh 'Canadian') and of the Communist Party of Great Britain (Philip Spratt) and of Sohan Singh Josh, Mir Abdul Majid and Kedar Nath Sehgal. (The last four, all Communists, were to be among the 31 accused in the Meerut Conspiracy Case in 1929-AD.) Intended to be a Workers and Peasants Party, it was named the Punjab Kirti-Kisan Party. Its organ Kirti was published in Punjabi and Urdu so that it could be read by the masses...Bhagat Singh worked for some time, assisting Sohan Singh Josh."

SECULARISM

Two of the six rules of the NBS drafted by Bhagat Singh were: "To have nothing to do with communal bodies or other parties which disseminate communal ideas" and "to create the spirit of general toleration among the public considering religion as a matter of personal belief of man and to act upon the same fully." Secularism was, indeed, an article of faith with Bhagat Singh all his life. Bipan Chandra described it thus: "More than any other contemporary leader, with the exception of Gandhiji, he understood the danger that communalism posed to Indian society and Indian nationalism. He often warned his comrades and followers that communalism was as big an enemy as colonialism...Religion, said Bhagat Singh, was the private concern of a person, but it had to be fought as an enemy when it intruded into politics and took the form of communalism. Bhagat Singh also believed that people must free themselves from the mental bondage of religion and superstition."

His classic article Why I am an Atheist is, of course, the most remarkable exposition of his approach to God and religion, which goes far beyond secularism and towards Marxism. The Hindi edition of The Complete Works of Bhagat Singh edited by Chaman Lal, comprises three very significant articles that were published in the Punjabi and Urdu monthly Kirti in May and June 1928.

The titles of these three articles are: Religion and Our Freedom Struggle; Communal Riots and their Solution; and The Problem of Untouchability. For reasons of space, it is not possible to quote from them here; suffice it to say that they are an extremely mature and forthright exposition of secularism and social justice. Remarkably, they were written when Bhagat Singh was just 21 years old.

Bipan Chandra, in India's Struggle for Independence, has cited the following revealing anecdote that throws light on Bhagat Singh's deep commitment to secularism: "Bhagat Singh revered Lajpat Rai as a leader. But he would not spare even Lajpat Rai, when, during the last years of his life, Lajpat Rai turned to communal politics. He then launched a political-ideological campaign against him. Because Lajpat Rai was a respected leader, he would not publicly use harsh words of criticism against him. And so he printed as a pamphlet Robert Browning's famous poem, 'The Lost Leader,' in which Browning criticizes Wordsworth for turning against liberty. The poem begins with the line 'Just for a handful of silver he left us.' A few more of the poem's lines were: 'We shall march prospering,-not thro' his presence; Songs may inspirit us,-not from his lyre' and 'Blot out his name, then, record one lost soul more.' There was not one word of criticism of Lajpat Rai. Only, on the front cover, he printed Lajpat Rai's photograph!"

MAIN CURRENTS IN THE NATIONAL MOVEMENT

The freedom of India from nearly two centuries of oppressive and exploitative British colonial rule was the cumulative result of a complex mosaic of four different currents that coexisted, often confronted and sometimes coordinated with one another. These were:

1. The current of armed struggles and peasant revolts that began with the Sannyasi-Fakir rebellion of 1760, encompassed the First War of Indian Independence of 1857, included the several groups of valiant armed freedom fighters throughout the country and ended with the revolt of the Royal Indian Navy ratings in 1946. All these armed struggles and peasant revolts were brutally crushed by the British, but some of them succeeded in shaking the British Raj to its roots.
2. The Indian National Congress, led by Mahatma Gandhi, which managed to establish its hegemony over the national movement after 1920. While the Congress succeeded in mobilizing millions of the Indian people in nonviolent upsurges against British rule, its bourgeois-landlord class leadership saw to it that these upsurges never crossed the boundary line to a radical agrarian revolution. Class struggle was, of course, anathema to the Congress, but it did adopt a broadly secular approach.
3. The Communist Party of India, which was formed in 1920, was the first to advocate the goal of complete independence in the Ahmedabad Congress session in 1921. Braving ban orders and massive repression of the British, the Communists plunged into the freedom movement and also organized workers and peasants for heroic class struggles, the pinnacle of which was the Telangana armed peasant revolt. Staunchly secular, the Communists were also the first to put forth the goal of socialism.
4. The social reform movement against caste and gender oppression that was led in various parts of the country by stalwarts like Raja Rammohan Roy, Mahatma Jotirao Phule, Ishwarchandra Vidyasagar, Narayan Guru, E V Ramaswamy Naicker (Periyar) and Dr. Babasaheb Ambedkar. The social reformers fought for freedom with social justice as one of its cardinal planks, an end to centuries of inhuman social oppression and the annihilation of the caste system itself.

There was a fifth current as well, but it was ranged directly against the national movement. This was the current of communalism. Not only did it never oppose the colonial rulers, but on the contrary it consistently helped British imperialism to execute its 'Divide and Rule' policy. It was represented by the Muslim League on the one hand, and by the RSS and the Hindu Mahasabha on the other. This current was socially reactionary, it led to constant communal clashes and it eventually resulted in the violent partition of India on the one hand, and in the dastardly assassination of Mahatma Gandhi on the other.

THE DISTINCTIVENESS OF BHAGAT SINGH AND HIS COMRADES

Bhagat Singh and his comrades belonged to the first current of armed anti-imperialist fighters. Their glorious struggle against British imperialism assumed legendary proportions. But their truly distinctive feature was that, amongst the large galaxy of thousands of armed freedom fighters spread over two centuries of the freedom struggle, it was Bhagat Singh and his comrades alone who were inexorably moving ideologically towards the third current-of Marxian socialism and the Communist Party. It is therefore no accident that comrades of Bhagat Singh like Shiv Verma, Kishori Lal, Ajoy Ghosh, Bejoy Kumar Sinha and Jaidev Kapur became leaders of the Communist movement after their release from British jails.

Bhagat Singh and his colleagues were also conscious of the need for social justice and the overthrow of the caste system. They were bitter and uncompromising enemies of communalism in all its forms. And they were inveterate opponents of the bourgeois-landlord class strategy and tactics of the Congress Party and its leadership that were exhibited in ample measure throughout the course of the national movement.

The distinctiveness of Bhagat Singh in the revolutionary firmament of the national movement has been well captured by B.T. Ranadive in his Foreword to the Selected Writings of Shaheed Bhagat Singh edited by Shiv Verma. He writes:

The name of Bhagat Singh and his comrades has secured a permanent place in the minds of the Indian people. No other revolutionary of those days struck such a deep feeling of sympathy, solidarity and oneness among the people. Bhagat Singh and his comrades became part of the people's consciousness, the symbol of their aspirations and prestige, the symbol of the fight to put an end to enslavement....

Punjab, Bengal and to some extent Maharashtra had earlier seen a large number of revolutionaries with unparalleled courage and capacity for self-sacrifice. They walked to the gallows with their head erect; they braved the horrors of the Andamans for years with unbending spirit. Their memory is no doubt cherished.

But they were challenging the empire at a time when the Indian masses had yet to move into political action. Their sacrifices did not become part of the common consciousness of the vast multitude that faced British lathis and rifles during the national movement in the succeeding years. On the other hand, Bhagat Singh and his comrades were in action when the masses were on the move, when every anti-British action drew their approbation. Their ultimate sacrifice, therefore, put a permanent impress on the consciousness of the Indian people...

Bhagat Singh went on churning his thoughts and proceeded more and more towards a better understanding of the Marxist stand on the issues facing the country. It may be stated without contradiction that his opinion on many national issues, his estimation of the national leadership and its weaknesses, were more or less in conformity with the views and opinions of the leaders of the Communist movement who were building their strength among the workers. His writings on various topics and his letters to his colleagues reveal his growing reliance on the Marxist outlook. It is no surprise that he declared himself an atheist and poured ridicule on the concept of a world created by a Supreme Being. His writings show a remarkable ability to merge with the subject under discussion and grasp the essence of points of dispute. They are permeated with an unfathomable sense of dedication to the cause of independence and freedom, to the cause of socialism. His study of Communist literature, of Lenin, led him to understand that India's struggle for freedom was part of the international working class struggle for socialism.

Pattabhi Sitaramayya, the official historian of the Congress, wrote that "it is no exaggeration to say that at that moment Bhagat Singh's name was as widely known all over India and was as popular as Gandhi's." In the same vein, a confidential Intelligence Bureau report of the British government, Terrorism in India (1917-1936) declared about Bhagat Singh that "for a time, he bade fair to oust Mr. Gandhi as the foremost political figure of the day."

A.G. Noorani concludes his book The Trial of Bhagat Singh-Politics of Justice with the words: "What distinguished Bhagat Singh from all others, besides his courage, patriotism and commitment to moral values, was his intellectual strength. A voracious reader, he was also willing to rethink. He had the capacity to brood and to torment his soul over the past. That led him to renounce terrorism, and to advise the young to follow suit; indeed, to counsel moderation and readiness to compromise. He was only 23 when he was hanged. On his death, Indian leaders vied with one another in lavishing praise on him. One wonders how many of them knew then that they had lost a man who, had he lived, might have had an incalculable impact on the course of India's politics."

HINDUSTAN SOCIALIST REPUBLICAN ASSOCIATION

Hindustan Socialist Republican Association (HSRA) was a revolutionary organisation, also known as the Hindustan Socialist Republican Army, established in 1928 at Feroz Shah Kotla in New Delhi by Chandrasekhar Azad, Bhagat Singh, Sukhdev Thapar and Ramprasad Bismil . Previously it was known as the Hindustan Republican Association (HRA), whose written constitution and published manifesto titled *The Revolutionary* were produced as evidence in the Kakori conspiracy case of 1925.

Origins

The Non-cooperation movement of 1920 led to large scale mobilisation in Indian population against the British rule. Though intended as a Nonviolent resistance movement, it soon turned violent. After the Chauri Chaura incident, Mahatma Gandhi suspended the movement to prevent escalation of violence. This disillusioned a section of nationalists who felt the suspension was premature and unwarranted. The political vacuum created by the suspension led to the formation of revolutionary movements by the more radical amongst those who sought to overthrow British rule.

Opposition of Gandhi in Gaya Congress

In February 1922 some agitating farmers were killed in Chauri Chaura by the police. Consequently,the police station of Chauri Chaura was attacked by the people and 22 policemen were burnt alive.

Without ascertaining the facts behind this incident, Mohandas K. Gandhi, better known as Mahatma Gandhi,declared an immediate stop the non-cooperation movement(he himself had given a call for it) without consulting any executive committee member of the Congress. Ram Prasad Bismil and his group of youth strongly opposed Gandhi in the Gaya Congress of 1922. When Gandhi refused to rescind his decision, the Indian National Congress was divided into two groups – one liberal and the other for rebellion. In January 1923, the liberal group formed a new Swaraj Party under the joint leadership of Moti Lal Nehru and Chittranjan Das, and the youth group formed a revolutionary party under the leadership of Bismil.

Yellow Paper constitution

With the consent of Lala Har Dayal, Bismil went to Allahabad where he drafted the constitution of the party in 1923 with the help of Sachindra Nath Sanyal and another revolutionary of Bengal, Dr. Jadugopal Mukherjee. The basic name and aims of the organisation were typed on a *Yellow Paper* and later on a subsequent Constitutional Committee Meeting was conducted on 3 October 1924 at Cawnpore in the United Provinces under the chairmanship of Sanyal.

Sharing responsibility

This meeting decided the name of the party would be the Hindustan Republican Association (HRA). Bismil was declared the

District Organiser for Shahjahanpur and Chief of Arms Division, as well as Provincial Organiser of United Province (Agra and Oudh). Sachindra Nath Sanyal became National Organiser and another senior member, Jogesh Chandra Chatterjee, was Coordinator of the Anushilan Samiti.

After attending the meeting in Kanpur, both Sanyal and Chatterjee left the United Provinces and proceeded to Bengal for further extension of the organisation.

The HRA established branches in Agra, Allahabad, Benares, Cawnpore, Lucknow, Saharanpur and Shahjahanpur. They also manufactured bombs in Calcutta – at Dakshineswar and Shovabazar – and at Deoghar in jharkhand . The Calcutta workshops were discovered by the police in 1925 and those in Deoghar were found in 1927.

Publication of Revolutionary

Sanyal wrote a manifesto for the HRA entitled *Revolutionary*. This was distributed around large cities of North India on 31 December 1924. It proposed the overthrow of British colonial rule and its replacement with what it termed a "Federal Republic of the United States of India". In addition, it sought universal suffrage and the socialist-oriented aim of abolition of "all systems which make any kind of exploitation of man by man possible"

The policies of Gandhi were criticised and youths were called to join the organisation. The police were astonished to see the language used and sought its leader in Bengal. Sanyal had gone to despatch this pamphlet in bulk and was arrested in Bankura, West Bengal. Before Sanyal's arrest, Jogesh Chandra Chatterjee had also been caught by police at Howrah railway station of Calcutta, Bengal.

Early activities

From 1924 to 1925, the HRA grew in numbers with the influx of new members like Bhagat Singh, Chandrasekhar Azad and Sukhdev Thapar.

There were many early attempts at disruption and obtaining funds, such as the robbery of a post office in Calcutta and of monies belonging to a railway at Chittagong, both in 1923, but the Kakori train robbery was the most prominent of the early HRA efforts. The Kakori event occurred on 9 August 1925, when HRA members looted government money from a train around 14 miles (23 km) from Lucknow and accidentally killed a passenger in the process.

Significant members of the HRA were arrested and tried for their involvement in that incident and others which had preceded it. The outcome was that four leaders – Ashfaqullah Khan, Ram Prasad Bismil, Roshan Singh and Rajendra Lahiri – were hanged in December 1927 and a further 16 imprisoned for lengthy terms.

The result of the trial, in which the HRA participants sang patriotic songs and displayed other forms of defiance, seriously damaged the leadership of the HRA and dealt a major blow to its activities.

Many associated with the HRA who escaped trial found themselves placed under surveillance or detained for various reasons. Azad was the only one of the principal leaders who managed to escape arrest.

Hindustan Socialist Republican Association

In 1928, the British government set up the Commission, headed by Sir John Simon, to report on the political situation in India. Some Indian activist groups protested the Commission, because it did not include a single Indian in its membership, although by no means all did so.

The effect was to galvanise various activist factions in opposition to a common cause.

Responding to the rise in anti-colonial sentiment in 1928, the HRA became the Hindustan Socialist Republican Association, with the change of name probably being largely due to the influence of Bhagat Singh.

Around the time of the Kakori robbery and the subsequent trial, various revolutionary groups had emerged in places such as Bengal, Bihar and Punjab. These groups and the HRA met at Feroz Shah

Kotla, in Delhi, on 7–8 August 1928, and from this emerged the HSRA. The socialist leanings voiced in the earlier HRA manifesto had gradually moved more towards Marxism and the HSRA spoke of a revolution involving a struggle by the masses to establish "the dictatorship of the proletariat" and the banishment of "parasites from the seat of political power".

It saw itself as being at the forefront of this revolution, spreading the word and acting as the armed section of the masses. Its ideals were apparent in other movements elsewhere at that time, including incidents of communist-inspired industrial action by workers and the rural kisan movement.

At the request of Bhagat Singh, the newly-named HSRA resolved to bomb members of the Simon Commission and also to cease robbing rich people, the latter being a realisation that the Kakori conspirators had suffered most from the evidence given by such people.

The HSRA's manifesto titled *Philosophy of the Bomb* was written by Bhagwati Charan Vohra.

Killing of John Saunders

When the Simon Commission visited Lahore on 30 October 1928, Lala Lajpat Rai led a peaceful protest against the Commission. The police responded with violence, with the superintendent of police, James A. Scott, ordering his men to *lathi* charge the protesters. Rai was beaten but addressed a meeting later.

He died on 17 November 1928, perhaps in part because of his injuries although this is uncertain. Historian Neeti Nair says "His death was widely attributed to the mental if not physical shock he had suffered."

When the matter of Rai's death was raised in the British Parliament, the government denied any casual role. Although Singh did not witness the event, he vowed to take revenge, and joined other revolutionaries, Shivaram Rajguru, Sukhdev Thapar and Chandrashekhar Azad, in a plot to kill Scott. However, in a case of mistaken identity, Singh was signalled to shoot on the appearance of John P. Saunders, an Assistant Superintendent of Police. He was shot by Rajguru and Singh while leaving the District Police Headquarters in Lahore on 17 December 1928. Chanan Singh, a Head Constable who was chasing them, was fatally injured by Azad's covering fire.

This case of mistaken identity did not stop Singh and his fellow-members of the HSRA from claiming that retribution had been exacted. The next day the HSRA acknowledged the assassination by putting up posters in Lahore that read

JP Saunders is dead; Lala Lajpat Rai is avenged. ... In this man has died an agent of the British authority in India. ... Sorry for the bloodshed of the human being, but the sacrifice of individuals at the altar of revolution ... is inevitable. The perpetrators of the Saunders murder having eluded capture and gone into hiding, the next major action by the HSRA was the bombing of the Central Legislative Assembly in Delhi on 8 April 1929.

This was a provocative propaganda exercise, intended to highlight the aims of the HSRA and timed as a protest against the introduction of the Public Safety Bill and the Trade Disputes Bill, both of which had been drafted in an attempt to counter the effects of revolutionary activities and trade unionism

Bhagat Singh and Batukeshwar Dutt threw bombs at the empty treasury benches, being careful to ensure that there were no casualties in order to highlight the propagandist nature of their action. They made no attempt to escape and courted arrest while shouting *Inquilab Zindabad* (Long Live the Revolution) and *Samrajyavad ka nash ho'* (Down with Imperialism). Their rationale for the bombing was explained in a leaflet titled "To Make the Deaf Hear" (paraphrasing the words of Édouard Vaillant). This leaflet was also thrown in the assembly and was reproduced the next day in the *Hindustan Times*. On 15 April 1929 police raided the HSRA's bomb factory in Lahore and arrested Kishori Lal, Sukhdev Thapar and Jai Gopal. The Assembly Bomb case trial followed and Bhagat Singh, Sukhdev and Rajguru were hanged on 23 March 1931 for their actions.

Later activities

In December 1929, the HSRA bombed the special train of Viceroy Irwin. The viceroy escaped unhurt. Later the Lahore faction of HSRA broke away and formed the *Atishi Chakar* (The Ring of Fire) party under the leadership of Hansraj . They carried out a series of bombings across Punjab in June 1930. On 1 September 1930, the Rawalpindi faction made a failed attempt to burgle the Office of the Controller of Military Accounts. During this period the leading members of the HSRA were Azad, Yashpal, Bhagwati Charan Vohra and Kailash Pati. In July 1930 the HSRA robbed the Gadodia stores in New Delhi and carried away 14,000 rupees. This money was later used to fund a bomb factory. In December 1930, an attempt was made to assassinate the Governor of Punjab, which wounded him in his arm.

Decline

By 1931, most of the HSRA's main leaders were either dead or in jail. Kailash Pati was arrested in October 1930 and turned approver (witness for the prosecution). On 27 February 1931, Chandrasekhar Azad shot himself during a gunfight with the police in a famous incident of Alfred Park. Bhagat Singh, Sukhdev Thapar and Rajguru were hanged in March 1931. After Azad's death there was no central leader to unite the revolutionaries and regional differences increased. The organisation split into various regional groups and they carried out bombings and attacks on Indian officials without any central coordination. In December 1931 another attempt was made to revive the HSRA at a meeting in Meerut. However this attempt failed with the arrests of Yashpal and Daryao Singh in 1932. This effectively ended the HSRA as a united organisation though the various regional factions kept up their armed struggle till 1936.

Criticism

The association's methods were diametrically opposite to that of Gandhi's nonviolent resistance movement. The revolutionaries and their methods were severely criticised by Gandhi. Responding to the attack on Lord Irwin's train, Gandhi wrote a harsh critique of the HSRA titled "The Cult of the Bomb" (*Young India*, 2 January 1930). In it he declared that bomb throwing was nothing but "froth coming to the surface in an agitated liquid". He condemned the HSRA and its actions as "cowards" and "dastardly". According to Gandhi, the HSRA's violent struggle had its hazards. Violence led to more reprisals and suffering. Also, it would turn inward as "it was an easy natural step" from "violence done to the foreign ruler" "to violence to our own people". The HSRA responded to this criticism with its own manifesto "The Philosophy of the Bomb", in which they defended their violent methods as being complementary to Gandhi's non-violent methods.

Legacy

A bomb factory and hideout located in Turi Bazaar, Firozpur, has been declared as a national monument by the Government of Punjab..

4

Batukeshwar Dutt and Defence of India Act 1915

THE UNSUNG BRAVEHEART WHO LAUNCHED SMOKE BOMBS ALONGSIDE BHAGAT SINGH

"At the appointed time, Bhagat Singh and BK Dutta threw the bombs over the empty seats in the Central Assembly, threw the historic pamphlets 'To Make the Deaf Hear' and shouted slogans: 'Inquilab Zindabad' and 'Samrajyavaad ka naash ho'."

On 8 April 1929, members of the Central Legislative Assembly had gathered together and begun their regular discussions, when suddenly, a strange object flew from the visitor's gallery and landed in an empty space in the hall.

Within moments, smoke started filling the area and shouts of "Inquilab Zindabad" (long live the revolution) were heard. Following this, the two men who had bombed the hall began to throw leaflets that carried the slogan, "It takes a loud sound to make the deaf hear."

Given the scare that the bomb had created, members of the assembly were running helter-skelter. The bombers, Bhagat Singh and Batukeshwar Dutt, could have easily escaped in the commotion, but they stayed—the bomb wasn't an empty threat. They wanted to make their voices heard.

Bhagat Singh is a widely celebrated revolutionary who inspired generations of youngsters during his time and continues to do so today. Unfortunately, Dutt, who was just as much a part of the legendary bombing as Singh, has remained an unsung hero.

Batukeshwar Dutt, fondly known as BK Dutt, Mohan or Battu was born on 18 November 1910 in the Oari village in what is now West Bengal.

He shifted to Kanpur to study in the PPN High school, from where he graduated. In 1924, Dutt met Bhagat Singh, and the two became thick friends. Bhagat Singh was an active member of the Hindustan Socialist Republican Association (HSRA) when he met Dutt, and soon, the latter joined the force too. Like Singh and Chandrashekhar Azad, Dutt learned how to make bombs during this time.

When the British Government passed the Defence of India Act, 1915, it gave them the undisputed power to control revolutionaries and their activities. HSRA declared their staunch opposition to the act, and Lala Lajpat Rai's death in a lathi charge further infuriated the association.

These events eventually led the HSRA to make a plan to bomb the Central Legislative Assembly. Singh and Dutt never wanted to escape. They readily accepted imprisonment, as they believed that it would inspire the next generation of revolutionaries to fight for the cause of freedom.

In fact, several years later, Asaf Ali, the lawyer who represented Dutt in the bombing case, revealed in an interview that Dutt had not actually thrown a bomb that day. He wanted to stay with Singh from the beginning to the end, so he allowed himself to be arrested.

Both the revolutionaries were sentenced for transportation for life (convicts were deported from mainland India for the remainder of their lives) in this case for "causing explosions of a nature likely to endanger life, unlawfully and maliciously." Singh was sent to the Mianwali Jail and Dutt, to the Central Jail in Lahore. Soon, Singh was transferred to the same jail that Dutt was in.

Here, they realised that they were treated like criminals, not political prisoners. Their European counterparts were treated with dignity and were provided with good food, clothes, books and newspapers. On the other hand, Indian political prisoners were made to perform undignified labour.

Furious with the treatment being meted out to them, they wrote an impassioned letter to the government of India, stating, stating that their diet needed to be better, and of the same standard as that of European prisoners. They also demanded that they be given "at least one standard daily paper, and "all books, other than those proscribed, along with writing materials, without any restriction."

You can read the entire text of the letter, here. The two revolutionaries sat on a legendary hunger strike to demand these rights from the British authorities and succeeded in securing some of them.

Many political prisoners were released by the British before they served their sentence if that meant appeasing the public. While Singh was hanged to death for shooting British officer John Saunders, Dutt was released from jail a few years later. He was in the Kalapani cellular jail in Andaman when he was released and had unfortunately contracted tuberculosis.

But that did not slow him down in any way. As soon as he was released, Dutt joined the Quit India movement initiated by Mahatma Gandhi. This earned him jail time, once again.

Five years later, India finally achieved independence from colonial rule. Even as several freedom fighters were honoured across the country, Dutt did not get his due, even though there was clear evidence of his involvement in the struggle.

Forced to live in dire poverty and without a government job, Dutt passed away in the AIIMS hospital in Delhi in 1965 and was cremated at the same spot where his comrades, Bhagat Singh, Rajguru and Sukhdev were cremated several years ago. Somewhere between the legendary bombing incident and India finally achieving its dream of independence, Dutt's story got lost.

A friend so loyal that he told a lie which sent him to prison, and a revolutionary so fierce that he participated in the freedom movement even when he had contracted a dreaded disease, BK Dutt undoubtedly deserves greater respect and recognition.

DEFENCE OF INDIA ACT 1915

The Defence of India Act 1915, also referred to as the Defence of India Regulations Act, was an emergency criminal law enacted by the Governor-General of India in 1915 with the intention of curtailing the nationalist and revolutionary activities during and in the aftermath of the First World War. It was similar to the British Defence of the Realm Acts, and granted the Executive very wide powers of preventive detention, internment without trial, restriction of writing, speech, and of movement. However, unlike the English law which was limited to persons of hostile associations or origin, the Defence of India act could be applied to any subject of the King, and was used to an overwhelming extent against Indians.

The passage of the act was supported unanimously by the non-official Indian members in the Viceroy's legislative council, and was seen as necessary to protect against British India from subversive nationalist violence. The act was first applied during the First Lahore Conspiracy trial in the aftermath of the failed Ghadar Conspiracy of 1915, and was instrumental in crushing the Ghadr movement in Punjab and the *Anushilan Samiti* in Bengal.

However its widespread and indiscriminate use in stifling genuine political discourse made it deeply unpopular, and became increasingly reviled within India. The extension of the law in the form of the Rowlatt Act after the end of World War I was opposed unanimously by the non-official Indian members of the Viceroy's council. It became a flashpoint of political discontent and nationalist agitation, culminating in the Rowlatt Satyagraha. The act was re-enacted during World War II as Defence of India act 1939. Independent India retained the law in a number of amended forms, which have seen use in proclaimed states of national emergency including Sino-Indian War, Bangladesh crisis, The Emergency of 1975 and subsequently the Punjab insurgency.

Background

Punjab and Bengal, along with Maharashtra, became hotbeds of revolutionary nationalist violence against British rule in India in the first decade of the 20th century. 1905 partition of Bengal and the 1907 colonisation bill in Punjab fed growing discontent. In Bengal, revolutionary organisations like *Anushilan Samiti* and *Jugantar* drew young recruits from the educated middle-class *Bhadralok* ranks, and engaged in a number of prominent attacks on both figures in the administration as well as the local police investigating incidents of robbery, violence and murder linked to these groups.

These included assassinations and attempted assassinations of civil servants, prominent public figures and Indian informants. In 1907 attempts were made on the life of the Bengal Lieutenant-Governor Sir Andrew Fraser. In 1908, a failed assassination attempt by *Jugantar* on the life of Presidency Magistrate Douglas Kingsford led to death of two European women.

In 1909, a failed assassination attempt saw two bombs thrown at Lord Minto. In December that year the magistrate of Nasik A. M. T. Jackson was shot dead by Anant Kanhere, and suspicion fell on links to India House in London which was at the time being led by V. D. Savarkar whose elder brother Ganesh had been convicted by Jackson of seditious conspiracy.

India House was also held responsible for the murder in London of William Hutt Curzon Wyllie, the political ADC to the secretary of state to India. A number of assassinations were also carried out of approvers who had turned crown-witnesses. In 1909 Naren Gossain, crown-witness for the prosecution in Alipore bomb case, was shot dead within Alipore Jail by Satyendranath Bose and Kanailal Dutt. Ashutosh Biswas, an advocate of Calcutta High Court in charge of prosecution of Gossain murder case, was shot dead within Calcutta High Court in 1909.

In 1910, Shamsul Alam, Deputy Superintendent of Bengal Police responsible for investigating the Alipore Bomb case, was shot dead on the steps of Calcutta High Court. In Punjab, agitation against the 1907 colonisation bill, which the protagonists falsely believed was attempting to introduce law of primogeniture. Punjab police had become aware of nuclei of nationalist movements arising across the state in the form of a nascent Ghadr movement, fed by resources and the efforts of emigrant Sikh communities living in Canada. Investigations during 1912 into an attempt to assassinate the then Viceroy of India, Charles Hardinge, promulgated the discovery of links between Bengal revolutionaries commanded by erstwhile Jugantar member Rash Behari Bose, and the Ghadr movement in Punjab.

Early laws

Preventive detention

The Bengal Regulation of 1812 and Regulation III of 1818 were some of the earliest laws in British India to incorporate the provisions of Preventive detention, without having to commit the detainee to trial. In the Presidencies of Madras and Bombay, similar laws had been enacted in 1819 and 1827 respectively. Prisoners under these regulations had no right of *habeas corpus*. Section 491 of the Criminal Procedure Code introduced the writ of Habeas Corpus in 1882. In 1907, emergency ordinances were issued in Punjab and in Eastern Bengal and Assam on the fiftieth anniversary of the 1857 mutiny. This allowed abolishment of public meetings, and the Indian press was subjected to controls to limit seditious material being published. The Explosive Substances Act and the Newspaper Act were passed in June 1908 to try and arrest agitation.

In June 1907 local governments were further authorised to initiate proceedings against local press publishing seditious material amongst civilian population or the army. *The Indian Sociologist* was banned in India in September 1907 and in November that year the Prevention of Seditious Meetings Act was passed. February 1910 saw the introduction of Indian Press Act which allowed Provincial governments to ask for punitive securities of up to Rs 5,000 from newspapers likely to incite sedition and violence. This act resulted in a number of nationalist publications closing down unable to provide such a surety.

Criminal law amendment 1908

Failure of prosecution in a number of cases under the Criminal procedures act 1898 led to a special act whereby crimes of nationalist violence were to be tried by a special tribunal composed of three high-court judges. December 1908 saw the passage of the Criminal Law amendments under the terms of Regulation III of 1818 and to suppress associations formed for seditious conspiracies. The act was first applied to deport nine Bengali revolutionaries to Mandalay prison in 1908. Despite these measures however, high standards of evidence demanded by the Calcutta High Court, insufficient investigations by police, and at times outright fabrication of evidence led to persistent failure to tame nationalist violence. Police forces felt unable to deal with the operations of secretive nationalist organisations, leading to demands for special powers. These were opposed vehemently in the Indian press, which argued against any extension of already wide powers enjoyed by the police forces in India, and which it was argued was being used to oppress Indian people.

World War I

The First World War began with an unprecedented outpouring of support towards Britain from within the mainstream political leadership, contrary to initial British fears of an Indian revolt. India contributed massively to the British war effort by providing men and resources. About 1.3 million Indian soldiers and labourers served in Europe, Africa and the Middle East, while both the Indian government and the princes sent large supplies of food, money and ammunition. However, Bengal and Punjab remained hotbeds of anti colonial activities. After the onset of the First World War, plague, rising grain prices, dissatisfaction with immigration policies within the British empire (highlighted by the *Komagata Maru* affair), and rumours of British misfortunes in the war meant by 1914, Punjab was in an unsettled state. India lay considerably far away from the Central Powers, with only feasible routes of invasion being through Persia and Afghanistan. The Indian Government at the outset of the war anticipated that India would remain safe as long as Afghanistan maintained neutrality, and the tribes of NWFP were under control. The worst situation would be from a combination of war with Afghanistan and internal unrest fomented by either the Bengali revolutionary network, the Ghadr in Punjab or Indian Muslims who may sympathise with Ottoman *Umma*.

Ghadr

British intelligence in North America indicated early in the war that the Ghadr Party, co-ordinating with the Berlin Committee in Germany, and the Indian revolutionary underground was attempting to transport men and arms from United States and East Asia into India, intended for a revolution and mutiny in the British Indian Army. From August 1914, a large number of Sikh expatriates began leaving Canada and USA under the plans of the Ghadr leadership for fomenting mutiny in India, whilst in Bengal nationalist crime also increased. Department of Criminal Intelligence chief Charles Cleveland noted that the threat to India should be dealt with by dealing with Ghadr activists who were already in India and those who were returning. To this end, Ingress into India Ordinance, 1914 was passed to limit the influx of Ghadarites, but failed to stem the inflow. The planned mutiny for February 1915 was averted at the last minute.

Bengal

In the meantime, the situation in Bengal worsened considerably following the Rodda Company raid by Jugantar, which handed large amount of firearms to Bengal revolutionaries. There were 36 outrages in 1915, climbing steeply from 13 in 1913 and 14 in 1914. The revolutionaries launched what has been described by some historians as "a reign of terror in both the cities and the countryside" that "came close to achieving their key goal of paralysing the administration." A general atmosphere of fear encompassed the police and the law courts, severely affecting the moral. In entire 1915, only six revolutionaries were successfully brought to trial.

Defence of India act

On 19 March 1915, Sir Reginald Craddock, home member in the Viceroy's council introduced the law and it passed in a single sitting. It was enacted as a temporary legislation in effect for the duration of World War I and for six months afterwards. The act gave the Governor General in Council the power to make rules for the purpose of securing the public safety and the defence of British India and as to the powers and duties of public servants and other persons in furtherance of that purpose...

Considerable pressure for the passage of the act was from Michael O'Dwyer particularly in light of the Ghadr threat. Answering to Sir Surendranath Bannerjee in the legislative assembly, Craddock denied any necessity or propriety for the government to constitute an advisory board of judicial character that would deal with the applications of the act. In this regard the law differed from the Defence of the Realm act. Craddock explained to the assembly that the lack of judicial oversight and advice were acceptable since the restrictive measures in the act were "preventive and not punitive in measures".

Scope

The law was to be valid for the duration of the war and for six months thereafter "for public safety" and "the defence of British India". The main object of the law made it illegal to communicate with the enemy, obtaining information, spreading false reports, as well as any activities that the government saw prejudicial to the war effort. The act allowed local governments to make rules detain indefinitely, without representation, and to try by special tribunals persons "*reasonably suspected*" of being of hostile origin or acting in a manner prejudicial to the safety of the empire. committing or conspiring to commit crimes either described in the act, or crimes which maybe punishable by death, transportation or at least seven year imprisonment. Power of detention, unlike under DORA, was carried by subordinate officers. For Trials already initiated under the Criminal procedures act 1898 or the 1908 Criminal law amendment were exempt from the act. Prosecution was to follow the procedures prescribed in the criminal procedures act 1898, but was superseded by the special powers and discretion of court. Crucially however, the Commissioners could take direct cognisance of the offences alleged and therefore preliminary procedures could be disposed off with.

Implementation

The act gave powers to local government to appoint three commissioners for trials who may be below the status of high-court judges. At least two would be Sessions judges or additional sessions judges for at least three years, were qualified for appointment as Judges of a High Court, or advocates of a Chief Court or pleaders of ten years' standing. A majority verdict was acceptable.

The act allowed the commissioners to accept as evidence statements recorded by a magistrates without scrutiny to cross examination and superseded the standards of evidence proscribed in the Indian evidence act 1872. Further the act allowed commissioners to accept such recorded evidence where the witness was unavailable or dead. This measure was intended to secure and safeguard against intimidation and assassinations by revolutionaries of approvers. There was no right to trial by jury. The act excluded from appeal or judicial review the decisions of the commissioners appointed under the Defence of India act.

Although designed to maintain order and curtail revolutionary movement, the law was in practice used in widespread scale from limiting revolutionaries, through arresting perpetrators of religious violence, to curtailing the voice of moderate political leaders. Unlike the Defence of the Realm Act (which was limited in scope to people of Hostile origin or associations, i.e. enemy citizens or collaborators), the act could be applied against any subject of the King. By June 1917, 705 were under home-arrest under the act, along with 99 imprisonments under Regulation III. Through the war, more than 1400 people were interned in India under the Defence of India Act alone, and a further three hundred subjected to minor restrictions, while more than two thousand were subjected to the restrictions of the Ingress into India Ordinance.

Impact

At the time of its enactment, the Defence of India act received universal support from Indian non-officiating members in the Governor General's council, from moderate leaders within Indian Political Movement. The British war effort had received popular support within India and the act received support on the understanding that the measures enacted were necessary in the war-situation. Its application saw a significant curtailment in revolutionary violence in India. However, the wide scope and widespread use amongst general population and against even moderate leaders led to growing revulsion within Indian population.

Revolutionary violence

The enactment of the law saw 46 executions and 64 life sentences handed out to revolutionaries in Bengal and Punjab in the Lahore Conspiracy Trial and Benares Conspiracy Trial, and in tribunals in Bengal, effectively crushing the revolutionary movement. The power of preventive detention were however applied more particularly to Bengal. By March 1916 widespread arrests helped Bengal Police crush the *Dhaka Anushilan Samiti* in Calcutta. Regulation III and Defence of India act was applied to Bengal from August 1916 on a wide scale. In Bengal, revolutionary violence in Bengal plummeted to 10 in 1917. By the end of the war there were more than eight hundred interned in Bengal under the act.

Moderate dissent

The application of the act was not limited to those suspected of revolutionary crimes. It gradually came to be used in coercing and suppressing the voice of many nationalist leaders, even of moderate views, where regional administration felt their opinion or views were seditious to British rule in India, or dangerous to the administration. A number of prominent moderate leaders were interned or deported under the Defence of India act. Most notable of these leaders was Mrs Annie Besant. Beasant had set up branches of the Home Rule League in major towns and cities at the time Bal Gangadhar Tilak was establishing the league in Bombay and in Western India. Although these amounted to little more than debating societies (having been modelled on the Fabian Societies), the leagues were noted to be publishing political pamphlets, selling alm ost 46000 of these in 1916. Libraries were also established where political treatises were made available. Beasant's league had 27000 members by 1917, and that same year both Tilak and Beasant were interned under the act on the grounds their activities were becoming subversive. India. Maulana Muhammad Ali Jauhar and Maulana Shaukat Ali were arrested and interned after they were found to have been in liaison with individuals in Kabul linked to the German mission, which the administration suspected may have been to promulgate a pan-Indian Islamic revolution. Abul Kalam Azad was deported from Bengal and placed under house arrest in Ranchi for his writing in *Al Balagh*.

Post-WWI

The Defence of India Act, in its implementation, was increasingly reviled. The unpopularity was such that the Lucknow session of the Indian National Congress in 1917 passed a resolution expressing alarm at the extensive use of the act, and urged the Government that its use be under same principles as the Defence of the Realm Act. Immediately after the war, Benjamin Horniman was deported from the Presidency of Bombay for his reporting on the Amritsar massacre.

Later laws

Rowlatt act

With the impending lapse of the 1915 act, the Rowlatt Committee was appointed to recommend measures to deal with the threat from the revolutionary movement. Rowlatt recommended an extension of the provisions of the Defence of India act for a further three years with removal of *habeas corpus* provisions. It was met with universal opposition by the Indian members of the Viceroy's council, as well within the population in general, earning the title of "The Black Bills" from Mohandas Gandhi. Mohammed Ali Jinnah left the Viceroy's council in protest, after having warned the council of the dangerous consequences of enacting an extension of such an unpopular bill. Rowlatt's recommendations were enacted in the Rowlatt Bills. The agitations against the proposed Rowlatt bills took shape as the Rowlatt Satyagraha under the leadership of Gandhi, one of the first Civil disobedience movements that he would lead the Indian independence movement. The protests saw hartals in Delhi, public protests in Punjab as well as other protest movements across India.

In Punjab, protests against the bills, along with a perceived threat of a Ghadrite uprising by the Punjab regional government culminated in the Jallianwalla Bagh Massacre in April 1919. After nearly three years of agitation, the government finally repealed the Rowlatt act and its component sister acts.

1939 act

The Defence of India act 1915 was re-enacted in a more severe form at the onset of World War II as the Defence of India act 1939. It was enacted on 29 September 1939 but deemed to come into force from 3 September 1939, the day when the Second World War began. The act was used notoriously during the war in subduing the independence movement. It expired six months after the termination of the war and was ultimately repealed by the Repealing and Amending Act,1947(Act II of 1948).

Independent India

The Indian Constitution retained the principles of preventive detention encapsulated in the Defence of India act, making one of the few countries were citizens of the country may be subjected to such measures. In Independent India, the law retained in legislations in the form of Preventive Detention act 1950, and has seen implementation as the Defence of India Rules 1962 during the Sino-Indian War of 1962, and the Defence of India Act,1971 during the 1971 Indo-Pak war. The 1962 act gained notoriety for its use in internment of Chinese immigrants in India, most notably Calcutta. Other similar laws enacted in independent India include the Maintenance of Internal Security Act (MISA) during *The Emergency*, and Terrorist and Disruptive Activities (Prevention) Act (enacted during the Punjab insurgency) which carry very similar provisions.

5

Batukeshwar Dutt and Bhagat Singh

Remembering our freedom fighters and revolutionaries who ensured independence always inspires us. However, there are some personalities whose stories are not often told and end up being lost with time.

One such story is of Batukeshwar Dutt, a revolutionary who was the bomb expert of Hindustan Socialist Republican Association (HSRA) in which the likes of Chander Shekhar Azad, Sardar Bhagat Singh, Ram Prasad Bismil, Ashfaqullah Khan, Roshan Lal, Sukhdev, Rajguru and many others were members.

Who can forget how Batukeshwar Dutt accompanied Bhagat Singh when the latter threw bombs in empty spaces in the Central Legislative Assembly, New Delhi on April 8, 1929. He could have escaped easily in the resulting mayhem but he stayed and shouted slogans against the British government.

While Bhagat Singh, Rajguru and Sukhdev were hanged on 23 March 1931, Dutt was sent to Kala Pani. He got freedom around 1942. After India got independence, Dutt kept approaching the government for a respectable employment for him, but the government didn't give him any job. He died helplessly in the lack of resources in AIIMS Delhi.

Dutt died an unknown and throughout his lives, he struggled to meet the ends despite sacrificing prime of his youth in Kala Pani and later during Quit India Movement. Here is the story of the great revolutionary:

Initial years

Batukeshwar Dutt aka BK, Battu and Mohan was born on 18 November 1910 to Goshtha Bihari Dutt in Oari village, Purba Bardhaman district. He graduated from PPM High School in Cawnpore where he came in touch with revolutionaries like Azad and Bhagat Singh.

Learnt how to make bombs

Being a member of HSRA, Dutt soon learnt how to make bombs in various secret places where HSRA used to hold meetings of the revolutionaries. It was he who made the bombs that were thrown by him and Bhagat Singh in the assembly in Delhi.

The bomb incident

On April 8, 1929, Bhagat Singh and Batukeshwar Dutt threw two bombs in empty space Central Legislative Assembly in New Delhi to protest against Defence of India Act 1915 implementation under which police were given free hand to nab any individual without any warrant or proof.

On 8 April 1929, Singh and Dutt threw two bombs inside the assembly rushing from Visitor's Gallery. The smoke from the bomb filled the hall and they shouted Inquilab Zindababd. Both could have escaped easily, but gave their arrest, so that the trial can give them the opportunity to connect with the people with the help media.

The leaflet claimed that the act was done to oppose the Trade Disputes and the Public Safety Bill being presented in the Central Assembly and the death of Lala Lajapath Rai.

Hunger strike in jail

Dutt along with Bhagat Singh, Sukhdev and several other revolutionaries initiated hunger strike in jail to protest against the abusive treatment of political prisoners by British. They succeeded in securing some rights for them as well.

"Without my companions, how can I eat? Let them come first. I will be absorbed in my book till then. I won't even know how the time passes,"Batukeshwar was quoted saying this during his hunger strike in the second volume of Indian Revolutionaries A Comprehensive Study, 1757-1961.

Sent to Kala Pani

While Bhagat Singh, Rajguru and Sukhdev were hanged in Lahore conspiracy case in which ASP Saunders was murdered by Rajguru. Dutt was sent on Andaman Cellular jail for the bombing Central Legislative Assembly in 1929. He was released from the jail in 1942.

But he participated in Quit India movement and sent to jail again

In 1942, he was released but soon again sent to jail because he actively participated in Quit Indian Movement started by Mahatma Gandhi. He had to spend another four years in jail.

India got freedom, but Dutt remained in oblivion

Dutt had contracted TB in jail and after Independence, he married in November 1947. He didn't get any recognition and despite him trying and seeking government help to get employed, he wasn't provided with any job. As a result, he was forced to start many businesses but all failed.

He died an unknown in AIIMS, Delhi

Dutt struggled to make ends meet and the prolonged disease of TB furthered drained up all the resources the family had. Dutt died an unknown after battling the long prolonged disease inthe paucity of the resources. Dutt outlived all his comrades and died on 20 July 1965 in the AIIMS hospital. He was cremated in Hussainiwala near Firozepur in Punjab where bodies of comrade friends Bhagat, Rajguru and Sukhdev were cremated many years before.

He was survived by his only child Bharti Bagchi. This is just one story of how India treated its freedom fighters and Dutt is relatively known figure yet he was accorded any recognition by government of India after independence, one can easily imagine the number of freedom fighters who's contribution was denied recognition by the very independent state they fought for.

REVOLUTIONARY BATTLES IN COURT AND JAIL

On June 12, 1929, the court sentenced Bhagat Singh and Batukeshwar Dutt in the Assembly Bomb Case to transportation for life in the Andamans. But in the meanwhile the police had uncovered the details of Saunders' assassination. Bhagat Singh, Rajguru, Sukhdev and several others were tried in the historic second Lahore Conspiracy Case. The trial started on July 10, 1929 and continued for over a year up to October 7, 1930.

Bhagat Singh and his comrades turned the court into a forum for revolutionary propaganda, just as the Communist undertrials were doing in the Meerut Conspiracy Case, which, significantly, was proceeding simultaneously with the Lahore Conspiracy Case. Both cases drew nationwide attention, but the Lahore Case was more in the limelight.

The revolutionaries began a prolonged hunger strike in jail to protest against the terrible jail conditions, to demand that they be treated not as ordinary criminals but as political prisoners, for necessities like proper diet, supply of books and newspapers and against forced labour.

The jail authorities did not relent and on September 13, 1929, on the 64th day of the hunger strike, Jatin Das died a martyr. A huge procession with his body was taken through the main roads of Lahore, culminating in a massive public meeting. His body was taken by train by Durga Bhabhi from Lahore to Calcutta and all along the route, thousands gathered at every station to pay him homage. In Calcutta itself, an unprecedented procession of more than six lakhs carried Jatin Das' coffin to the cremation ground.

Later, on May 17, 1933, Mahavir Singh, another comrade of Bhagat Singh who was transported for life in the Lahore Conspiracy

Case, was martyred in the indefinite hunger strike in the Andaman Cellular Jail.

On October 19, 1929, the second Punjab Students' Conference was held at Lahore under the presidentship of Subhash Chandra Bose. From jail, Bhagat Singh sent a short message to the Conference which was read out and received thunderous response. In this message Bhagat Singh said, "Comrades, Today, we cannot ask the youth to take to pistols and bombs. Today, students are confronted with a far more important assignment. In the coming Lahore Session the Congress is to give a call for a fierce fight for the independence of the country. The youth will have to bear a great burden in this difficult time in the history of the nation...The youth will have to spread this revolutionary message to the far corners of the country. They have to awaken the crores of slum-dwellers of the industrial areas and villagers living in worn-out cottages, so that we can become independent and the exploitation of man by man will become an impossibility." Students and Politics and Youth were two other articles written by Bhagat Singh, who always set great store by the youth.

The HSRA revolutionaries observed memorable days in the court itself. On December 19, 1929, they observed 'Kakori Day' and paid homage to their hanged comrades. On January 21, 1930, they appeared in the court wearing red scarves to celebrate Lenin Day. Bhagat Singh read out a telegram and asked the magistrate to send it to the Third International. The text was: "On Lenin Day we send hearty greetings to all who are doing something for carrying forward the ideas of the great Lenin. We wish success to the great experiment Russia is carrying out. We join our voice to that of the international working class movement. The proletariat will win. Capitalism will be defeated. Death to Imperialism." On May 1, 1930, they celebrated May Day and on November 7, 1930, they sent greetings to the Soviet Union on the anniversary of the Revolution.

The year 1930 saw several historic events in the freedom struggle. At the call of the Lahore Congress in December 1929, that for the first time belatedly adopted the goal of complete independence, January 26, 1930 was celebrated throughout the country as

Independence Day by raising the national flag. The mass civil disobedience movement began with the Dandi March and Salt Satyagraha of Mahatma Gandhi from March 12 to April 6, 1930. Millions participated in spontaneous demonstrations all over the country. This time, again, the movement did not always follow the Gandhian guideline of non-violence. More than 50 cases of 'terrorist' activities were registered in 1930. Some were extremely prominent.

On April 18, 1930, Surya Sen alias Masterda and his comrades Tarakeshwar Dastidar, Nirmal Sen, Ganesh Ghosh, Ananta Singh, Ambika Chakravarty, Loknath Bal, Kalpana Dutt, Pritilata Waddedar and the tiny Subodh Roy, of the Indian Republican Army (IRA) conducted the historic Chittagong Armoury Raid in Bengal and fought a pitched armed battle against the British. On April 23, 1930, Chandra Singh Garhwali and his Garhwali regiment, comprising Hindu soldiers, refused to fire on their Muslim Pathan brethren at Peshawar in the North-West Frontier Province. On May 7, 1930, the textile workers of Solapur in Maharashtra launched a general strike, drove out the British, took over the city and ran a parallel government for ten days up to May 16, when the British imposed Martial Law.

These acts met with fierce British repression. Surya Sen and Tarakeshwar Dastidar were hanged on January 12, 1934. Chandra Singh Garhwali was court-martialled and sentenced to death. His sentence was then commuted and he was sent to transportation for life along with many others. Four leaders of the Solapur revolt-Jagannath Shinde, Qurban Hussein, Malappa Dhanshetty and Srikisan Sarda were hanged on January 12, 1931.

May 28, 1930 was a tragic day for the HSRA. One of its tallest leaders and ideologues, Bhagwati Charan Vohra, was killed in an accident while testing a highly powerful bomb on the banks of the Ravi river. He was manufacturing these bombs to rescue Bhagat Singh and his comrades from jail. Before he died his last words to those accompanying him were, "Do not grieve over this accident. Remember, the task of rescuing Bhagat Singh and others still remains incomplete."

The death of Bhagwati Charan had a shattering effect on his wife, who was called Durga Bhabhi. Along with other HSRA comrades, she had herself earlier taken part in the daring Lamington Road police station shooting episode in Bombay. She continued her revolutionary activities for many more decades. Shiv Verma wrote in 1986, "Much of the work on this volume (Selected Writings of Shaheed Bhagat Singh) was done at Lucknow at Durga Bhabhi's place. The care, love and affection I received from her was another source of courage and inspiration."

When the case was in its final stage, on September 20, 1930, Bhagat Singh's father Kishan Singh made a written request to the Tribunal, saying that there were many facts to prove his son was innocent of Saunder's murder and that his son be given an opportunity to prove his innocence. Bhagat Singh was infuriated and wrote an open letter to his father on October 4, 1930, which was printed in the Tribune. The letter is historic and throws light on Bhagat Singh's revolutionary character:

My life is not so precious, at least to me, as you may probably think it to be. It is not at all worth buying at the cost of my principles. There are other comrades of mine whose case is as serious as that of mine. We had adopted a common policy and we shall stand to the last, no matter how dearly we have to pay individually for it. Father, I am quite perplexed. I fear I might overlook the ordinary principles of etiquette and my language may become a little bit harsh while criticizing or censuring this move on your part. Let me be candid. I feel as though I have been stabbed in the back. Had any other person done it, I would have considered it to be nothing short of treachery.

But in your case, let me say that it has been a weakness-a weakness of the worst type. This was the time when everybody's mettle was being tested. Let me say, father, that you have failed. I know you are as sincere a patriot as one can be. I know you have devoted your life to the cause of Indian independence, but why, at this moment, have you displayed such a weakness? I cannot understand. In the end, I would like to inform you and my other friends and all the people interested in my case, that I have not approved of your move. I want that the public should know all the details about this complication, and therefore, I request you to publish this letter. Your loving son, Bhagat Singh.

On October 7, 1930, the Special Tribunal in the Lahore Conspiracy Case delivered judgement convicting all the accused except three who were acquitted-Ajoy Kumar Ghosh, Jatindra Nath Sanyal and Des Raj. Bhagat Singh, Rajguru and Sukhdev were sentenced to death. Kishori Lal, Mahavir Singh, Bejoy Kumar Sinha, Shiv Verma, Gaya Prasad, Jaidev Kapur and Kamalnath Tewari were sentenced to transportation for life. Kundan Lal Gupta was sentenced to seven years; Prem Dutt, to five. Almost all these revolutionaries were in their twenties. The nation was stunned. It reverberated with the demand for the commutation of the death sentences on the heroic youth.

'OUR UNDISPUTED IDEOLOGICAL LEADER'

Before and after the judgement, Bhagat Singh's reading and writing in jail continued unabated. As he declared before the Lahore Court, "The sword of revolution is sharpened on the whetstone of ideas." Shiv Verma, in an interview given to the present writer in Mumbai on March 5, 1991, replied to a question as to what set Bhagat Singh apart from the others, as follows, "I can tell you that in just one sentence: Bhagat Singh was our undisputed ideological leader.

I do not remember a single moment when Bhagat Singh did not have a book in his pocket. The other virtues of Bhagat Singh like tremendous courage and so on were there in the other revolutionaries amongst us also. But his uniqueness lay in his great studiousness. The degree of clarity and integrity that he had about the aims of our movement, was not there in any one of us at that time." Bipan Chandra wrote that, "Bhagat Singh was already at a young age a giant of an intellectual and thinker." Chaman Lal wrote that, "Bhagat Singh had command of four languages, without much formal training or education. He wrote in Punjabi, Hindi, Urdu and English. His jail notebooks collect excerpts from 108 authors and 43 books including prominently Marx, Engels and Lenin, but also many others."

There are various volumes of the writings of Bhagat Singh compiled by Shiv Verma, Chaman Lal and Bhagat Singh's nephew Jagmohan Singh and his niece Virender Sindhu. They are a treasure house. There are also several meaningful letters written by him. For instance, he wrote a letter reprimanding Sukhdev who had said that if he did not get the death sentence, he would rather commit suicide than face life imprisonment. A month after he was given the death sentence, in November 1930 he wrote a letter to Batukeshwar Dutt in which he gave an idea of what he expected from comrades who had escaped capital punishment. 'Why I Am An Atheist' and 'Introduction to Dreamland' were two seminal tracts written by him in jail. It is the greatest of misfortunes that four other books written by Bhagat Singh in jail, viz.

The Ideal of Socialism, Autobiography, History of Revolutionary Movement in India and At the Door of Death, although they were smuggled out of jail, were later destroyed. The Statement of the Undefended Accused, drafted by Bhagat Singh, launched this scathing attack on imperialism, which can well apply even to the present situation in the world: "We believe that imperialism is nothing but a vast conspiracy organized with predatory motives.

Imperialism is the last stage of development of insidious exploitation of man by man and of nation by nation. The imperialists, with a view to further their piratical designs, not only commit judicial murders through their law courts but also organize general massacres, devastations and other horrible crimes like war. They feel no hesitation in shooting down innocent and unarmed people who refuse to yield to their depredatory demands or to acquiesce in their ruinous and abominable designs. Under the garb of custodians of 'law and order', they break peace, create disorder, kill people and commit all conceivable crimes."

Summing up his political thought, Bhagat Singh said in a message sent from prison in October 1930: "We mean by revolution the uprooting of the present social order. For this capture of state power is necessary. The state apparatus is now in the hands of the privileged class. The protection of the interests of the masses, the translation of our ideal into reality, that is, laying the foundation of society in accordance with the principles of Karl Marx, demand our seizure of this apparatus."

On February 2, 1931, less than two months before his martyrdom, Bhagat Singh wrote the remarkable appeal To Young Political Workers, which is his last testament. After analyzing the prevailing conditions and the tactics of the Congress, he advised youth to adopt Marxism as their ideology, work among the people, organize workers and peasants and join the Communist Party. He wrote: "We require-to use the term so dear to Lenin-the 'professional revolutionaries'. The whole time workers who have no other ambition or life-work except the revolution. The greater the number of such workers organized into the Party, the greater the chances of your success...The name of the Party should be the Communist Party. This Party of political workers, bound by strict discipline, should handle all other movements. It shall have to organize the peasants' and workers' parties, labour unions, and may even venture to capture the Congress and kindred political bodies. And in order to create political consciousness, not only of national politics but class politics as well, the Party should organize a big publishing campaign."

In the same appeal, renouncing terrorism, he wrote, "Apparently I have acted like a terrorist. But I am not a terrorist. I am a revolutionary who has got such definite ideas of a lengthy programme as is being discussed here...Let me announce with all the strength at my command, that I am not a terrorist and I never was, except perhaps in the beginning of my revolutionary career. And I am convinced that we cannot gain anything through those methods."

REVOLUTIONARY IMMORTALITY

On February 27, 1931, Chandrashekhar Azad, the Commander-in-chief of the HSRA, who was still at large, went to the Alfred Park at Allahabad. Along with Bhagat Singh, Chandrashekhar Azad was the most respected figure in the ranks of the revolutionaries. His courage and daring were legendary, and so also were his organizational skills. His classic marksmanship made him a terror for the British police. Despite the fact that he was not too well-educated, his political sharpness was amazing. With uncommon skill, he had eluded arrest by the police for years. But now he was betrayed by a traitor from within his own ranks and was surrounded. A fierce gun-fight with the police ensued in which Chandrashekahar Azad was killed. The life of another great revolutionary was snuffed out.

One of the negative features of the HSRA, which was common in most such underground revolutionary bodies, was the presence of traitors and approvers, who caused untold damage to the cause. In his pamphlet Bhagat Singh and his Comrades written in 1945, Ajoy Ghosh, one of the colleagues of Bhagat Singh who later became the General Secretary of the CPI from 1951-62, wrote of the time when several of them were arrested in the Lahore Conspiracy Case: "It all seemed over, our dreams and our hopes. More depressing than anything else was the shocking fact that, unable to stand police torture, no less than seven, two of them members of our central committee, had turned approvers."

One of these approvers and a former central committee member of HSRA was Phanindranath Ghosh. Since he had the most knowledge, his testimony proved to be the most damaging to Bhagat Singh and his comrades. As revenge, Phanindranath Ghosh was killed by Vaikuntha Shukla and Chandrama Singh on November 9, 1932. Shukla was hanged and Singh was consigned to long years of imprisonment.

A few days before his execution, in a letter written in March 1931 to the Punjab Governor, Bhagat Singh wrote, "Let us declare that the state of war does exist and shall exist so long as the Indian toiling masses and their natural resources are being exploited by a handful of parasites.

They may be purely British capitalists, or mixed British and Indian, or even purely Indian. They may be carrying on their insidious exploitation through mixed or even purely Indian bureaucratic apparatus. All these things make no difference...This war shall continue...It shall be waged with new vigour, greater audacity and unflinching determination till the socialist republic is established."

Referring to the unparalleled sacrifices of Jatin Das, Bhagwati Charan Vohra and Chandrashekhar Azad, he ended his letter pointing out to the Punjab Governor that since the verdict of the court was that they had waged war against the British empire, they were war prisoners; therefore "we claim to be shot dead instead of being hanged."

On March 22, the day before Bhagat Singh's execution, his comrades in jail sent him a slip asking if he would like to live. He wrote back: "The desire to live is natural.

It is in me also. I do not want to conceal it. But it is conditional. I don't want to live as a prisoner or under restrictions. My name has become a symbol of the Indian revolution. The ideals and the sacrifices of the revolutionary party have elevated me to a height beyond which I will never to be able to rise if I live... Yes, one thing pricks me even today. My heart nurtured some ambitions for doing something for humanity and for my country. I have not been able to fulfil even one thousandth part of those ambitions. If I live I might perhaps get a chance to fulfil them. If ever it came to my mind that I should not die, it came from this end only. I am proud of myself these days and I am anxiously waiting for the final test. I wish the day may come nearer soon. Your comrade, Bhagat Singh."

Manmathnath Gupta, who was sentenced in the Kakori case, has reconstructed the events of March 23, 1931, the last day in the life of Bhagat Singh, Rajguru and Sukhdev. The Chief Warder of the jail, one Chatar Singh, got the order in the afternoon that the hanging was to take place the same evening.

The God-fearing man approached Bhagat Singh and pleaded with him to pray and read a holy book that he had brought along. Bhagat Singh politely refused, saying that he had been an atheist all his life and would remain so even on this last day.

The whole day, Bhagat Singh was reading a biography of Lenin that had been sent to him at his express wish. When, at around seven in the evening, a jail official came to take him to the gallows, Bhagat Singh, still engrossed in reading Lenin's biography, said, "Wait a minute, one revolutionary is busy meeting another." After reading for a while, he got up and embarked on his final journey. Amidst slogans of 'Down With Imperialism' and 'Long Live Revolution', the three martyrs-Bhagat Singh, Rajguru and Sukhdev-attained revolutionary immortality. The final song on their lips was:

Dil se niklegi na markar bhi watan ki ulfat,

Meri mitti se bhi khushbue watan aaegi.

(Love for the motherland will not leave my heart even after death,

Its fragrance will still be there in my dusty remains.)

Drawing lessons from the massive crowds that had gathered for Jatin Das' funeral earlier, and apprehending an immeasurably greater uproar this time, the British authorities secretly took away all three bodies. Without handing them over to the relatives of the martyrs, the jail authorities hurriedly cremated them near Ferozepur on the banks of the Sutlej.

Bipan Chandra recounts: "The entire country went into mourning on hearing the news of their martyrdom. Angry condolence meetings and demonstrations were held in cities and towns, in which many who had earlier stood aside participated. In many places, demonstrators clashed with the police and faced firing and lathi charges in which over a hundred people died. Hundreds of schools and colleges observed hartals; lakhs fasted on that day."

Soon after the martyrdom of these three heroes, in the last week of March 1931 a serious communal riot broke out in Kanpur. The senior Congress leader Ganesh Shankar Vidyarthi, who was one of the mentors of Bhagat Singh and his comrades, was killed by fanatics while he was boldly trying to save the lives of innocents from communal wrath. This tragedy underlined Bhagat Singh's constant warnings against the grave danger of communalism.

AS REVOLUTIONARY

Bhagat Singh was just 23 years and a few months when he was hanged by British colonialists on March 23, 1931. By the time Bhagat Singh went to the gallows, he had entered the hearts and minds of all Indians, some of whom later became Pakistanis and Bangladeshis. With the publication of Bhagat Singh's writings largely after 1947 and more in the last few decades of twentieth century (complete documents in Hindi are now available in one volume), the martyr became known as a revolutionary socialist thinker as well. This year not only happens to be Bhagat Singh's 75th year of martyrdom but will also mark the beginning of his birth centenary year on September 28. Bhagat Singh was born on September 28, 1907, in Lyallpur Banga. His ancestral village, however, is Khatkarkalan near Banga in Nawanshahar district. Bhagat Singh spent most of his childhood in Pakistan's Punjab, particularly Lahore. He was also martyred in Lahore.

Bhagat Singh is revered not only in India but also in Pakistan and Bangladesh, while people in countries like Nepal, Sri Lanka also respect this great revolutionary from India.

Even in international arena, if Mahatma Gandhi has become a symbol of Indian nonviolent struggle for freedom, Bhagat Singh's name comes close to great revolutionaries like Che Guvera, Simon Bolivar and Nelson Mandela.

There is a need to propagate Bhagat Singh's ideas by translating his documents in all Indian languages. A picture of Bhagat Singh should be hung in Parliament. His writings against communalism and untouchability could be introduced in school curricula. This freedom fighter is a symbol of unity for the people of India, Pakistan and Bangladesh, and his ideas can be a beacon of light for them.

It is suggested that Bhagat Singh's martyrdom day should be observed as "Anti-Colonialism/Anti-Imperialism Day" in the subcontinent. It should be observed in a big way at Lahore by Indians and Pakistanis jointly. The main function should be held at Lahore Jail on March 23 at 7 pm, when 75 years ago he along with two other patriots Rajguru and Sukhdev were hanged by the British. Artists, activists and writers of both countries should hold a weeklong event, which could include seminars, street and stage plays and film shows. This would help revive the memories of the martyrs and spread their ideas among the youth

In fact, it is felt that Pakistan should enter into a healthy competition with India in claiming the legacy of Bhagat Singh. Bhagat Singh was born, brought up and educated in Pakistan. He had his revolutionary training in National College at Lahore. His activities in India include holding a meeting of revolutionaries at Delhi in September 1928 and dropping a bomb on the Central Assembly in Delhi, apart from spending sometime in Kanpur or some other places. The joint legacy of Bhagat Singh can help both countries come closer, at least culturally.

The birthday of Bhagat Singh (September 28) should be declared as "National Youth Day". The ideas of the martyr would enthuse the youth, who are the builders of the free nation.

This freedom fighter no longer remains an individual. Historical personalities become symbols of ideas and movements. Bhagat Singh has emerged as a symbol of the most radical nationalist movement against imperialism and colonialism. He represents the highest ideals of Indian revolutionary movement.

Bhagat Singh is one among many national heroes, whom Dalits and minorities-who form a large chunk of the Indian society-are ready to accept as their hero because of his radical views on untouchability and communalism. Along with Dr. Ambedkar, Bhagat Singh also has an appeal for Dalits of this nation.

In the context of misuse or overexposure of religion by some fascist fundamentalist groups in our society, Bhagat Singh's ideas on religion or atheism can work as an antidote to counter such pernicious views

All democratic and nationalist Indians should unite on this occasion and by focusing on Bhagat Singh's ideas, build a powerful resistance movement against a much more dangerous neo-colonial onslaught, more powerful than the old colonialist British empire.

BHAGAT SINGH-AN UNSUNG HERO

In a country dominated by the word "Gandhi", there are innumerable other unsung heroes of the freedom movement of this country.

One such hero is Shaheed Bhagat Singh.

Bhagat Singh (born on September 28, 1907) was one of the most famous youth revolutionaries of the Indian Independence Movement, who at the very young age of 13 was a part of Mahatma Gandhi's noncooperation movement against the British. Bhagat Singh was deeply affected by the 1919 Jallianwala Bagh Massacre and believed that violence should be replied back only by violence. He was also disappointed when Gandhi called back the noncooperation movement following the Chauri Chaura incident.

Bhagat Singh's freedom movement reached a turning point when the British killed the veteran activist Lala Lajpat Rai in a police lathi charge while he was leading a peaceful protest against the Simon's commission for not including any Indian representatives in the commission.

Lala Lajpat Rai succumbed to the injuries of the lathi charge within a month after the incident. Bhagat Singh was deeply hurt by the death of Lala Lajpat Rai and in a bid to take revenge he and other revolutionaries (Shivaram Rajguru, Sukhdev and Jai Gopal) plotted a bid to kill Scott, the police chief. However in a case of mistaken identity, they killed Saunder, a deputy superintendent of police. After that when the British Govt brought the Defence of India Act, giving more power to the police inspite of the act being voted down in the council by one vote, Bhagat Singh's organization decided to protest against this act by exploding non-lethal bomb in the corridors of the assembly and by throwing leaflets containing the message 'It takes a loud voice to make the deaf hear'. Singh and Batukeshwar Dutt executed these actions.

Following the explosions, Singh and Dutt, who were still in the corridors of the assembly chanting 'Inquilab Zindabad' were arrested. British also came to know about the assassination of Scott by him, and as a result the British Government hanged Bhagat Singh to death. Unfortunately, no real attempts were made by the nonviolent movement led by Gandhi to get Bhagat Singh and his associates released. Sukhdev who was also hanged along with Bhagat, had written a letter to Gandhi just before their hanging, protesting against Gandhi's disapproval of their revolutionary tactics. The same year/month (1931 March) in which Bhagat and his fellow comrades (Rajguru and Sukhdev) were hanged, Gandhi signed a pact with Lord Irwin, the then viceroy of India and got all his followers released, who were arrested by the British earlier for participating in Gandhi's civil disobedience movement.

A Radical Legacy

Bhagat Singh and associates radicalised the national movement by broadening its scope and creating space for popular interventions.

Bhagat Singh and his comrades belong to those momentous decades in Indian history-the late 1920s and 30s-when options were more open, popular aspirations ran high and "revolution" and "national liberation" were current in the political vocabulary and intrinsic to the national agenda of a well-defined stream within the national movement. They were among that remarkable set of people whose deeds made them natural heroes and who, by their words and actions, exposed the weaknesses of the national movement in those very years that it was becoming a mass movement. That in the process they also influenced it very deeply has largely been erased not just from official recordings of India's political heritage, but even in the general recalling of its history. Despite all the emphasis on people's history, current historiography on that period has simply failed to give them their due. It is time the record was set straight.

Bhagat Singh and his comrades-like all other progressive groups and individuals of the time-cannot be understood without reference to the historic impact of the Russian revolution of 1917 on India. No event before it had such an impact on the minds of the people in the colonies. Suddenly it seemed that it was possible to throw off the yoke of oppression. Nations could be free, sovereign and equal, and people within those nations could be free, sovereign and equal. National liberation, world revolution, popular interests and socialism could be talked of in one breath and this was the inspiration and the message of those decades. Bhagat Singh and his comrades and all other progressive, socialist and communist groups in the country were inspired by this heritage of the Russian revolution, and would not have done much of what they were able to without it. Among them no single individual did as much by his words and deeds in the late 1920s to communicate this message within the national movement as did Bhagat Singh.

It can be easily said that Bhagat Singh and his comrades and the organisations to which they belonged, the Naujawan Bharat Sabha and the Hindustan Socialist Republican Association, played a central and foundational role in popularising the left-radical agenda within the national movement and giving visibility to this agenda in the national political life of those years.

The few books brought out this year underline the fact that Bhagat Singh and his comrades were a significant stream within the left, and by their heroism and deeds played a central role in both broadening the scope of the Congress-led movements and in popularising the slogans and goals of the Communist movement in India. One cannot think that ideas of revolution and socialism could have become as popular as they did then, or that Gandhi could have felt the challenge that he did then, were it not for the political intervention of Bhagat Singh and his comrades and their firm alignment with Communist politics.

They left their impress on the Congress politics of their time. It is difficult to imagine a Congress 'Left' or the polarisation within the Congress without their activities and campaigns. It is they among the Communist groups who succeeded in creating an unease and embarrassment for Jawaharlal Nehru and Subhash Chandra Bose, which exposed the divergence between word and deed among the best of Congresspersons. They contributed to inspiring many to come out of the Congress, even as the more right-wing leadership of the Congress was upholding policies of the organisation that defended the class interests of the bourgeoisie and landlords.

The churning within the Congress was played out at all its conferences, where resolutions critical of the activities of Bhagat Singh and his comrades could be passed only by very thin majorities, and only at the personal insistence of Gandhi himself.

Bhagat Singh and his comrades publicly put forward a scathing critique of Gandhi and the Congress politics. They worked along with the Congress for a time as other Communists did, and pressured the leadership to adopt many resolutions that were beyond the scope of the Congress agenda or the Congress was not prepared to accept until then. This they did largely by their independent campaigns and examples of heroism, which the Congress could not match.

They participated wholeheartedly in the Non-Cooperation Movement, and members of the Naujawan Bharat Sabha and the Hindustan Socialist Republican Association manned the committees at the district, tehsil and taluka levels in many parts of north India during the Civil Disobedience Movement, infusing a more radical content into it.

They aligned these movements with slogans pertaining to peasants' and workers' demands. In this way, they broadened the scope and canvas of the national movement, and created space for popular interventions and initiatives.

They exposed the hollowness of the demand of dominion status for India and put forward the idea of complete independence and opposition to imperialism in general.

They formed the backbone of the popular mobilisations against the Simon Commission and political repression of the British. They went to the people with an alternative not only to Congress politics, but also its organisations. Bhagat Singh became as popular as Gandhi, and more popular than him among the youth. The revolutionaries' slogans and cries for revolution found an echo among all sections of people almost in all corners of the country. Every heart beat for them during the years of their trial, confinement and execution at the hands of the British. Gandhi's compromise with the British on their executions made him unpopular, and he was greeted with negative slogans and black flags wherever he went. Cries of revolution rent the air even in Congress platforms and conferences.

The gap between their ideological influence and organisational achievements is typical of the early stages of revolutionary and left movements throughout history, and does not detract from their contribution to national politics and national culture.

It is pertinent that the Hindustan Republican Association was formed in 1924 and its manifesto 'The Revolutionary' declared its commitment to secularism and revolution in 1925, precisely when Hindu communalism was consolidating itself in the form of the

Rashtriya Swayamsewak Sangh (RSS) and the Hindu Mahasabha. In 1926, the Hindustan Republican Association had transformed itself into the Hindustan Socialist Republican Association, by identifying itself with socialist ideals and laying claim to the heritage of the world communist movement.

At a time when the Congress allowed dual membership to RSS and Hindu Mahasabha members, the Hindustan Socialist Republican Association made a trenchant critique of religion and communal mobilisations. Even if they could not succeed in organising workers and peasants, they brought their issues into the consciousness of the youth.

They popularised new symbols and slogans in public fora and mass politics. They linked national liberation with revolution in the minds of large sections of youth.

Red flags became common and socialism became part of the vocabulary of the national movement. Cries of Vande Mataram and Bharat Mata were substituted by Hindustan Zindabad and Inquilab Zindabad. New traditions were created by them with pamphleteering, study circles and agitational programmes, and celebrations and commemorations of the Russian revolution, the Irish struggle, Kakori Day, May Day and Lenin Day.

They translated into popular propaganda the economic analysis of British imperialism by Dadabhai Nauroji and R.C. Dutt. They were in close touch with many members of the Communist Party, and provided public platforms to Congresspersons, both radicals such as Subhash Chandra Bose and others such as Nehru, and Communist Party members such as S.A. Dange and Philip Spratt. In doing all this, they radicalised the national movement.

The Naujawan Bharat Sabha and its offshoots were the first left-wing mass organisations to attain national fame and public visibility, which encouraged young people from middle class and lower middle class backgrounds to work for ideals that transcended their own class interests. They initiated campaigns and networks that created huge space for Left politics at a mass level, particularly in Punjab and United Provinces, and some other parts of north India. Their resolutions, deliberations, emphasis on study and struggle, anti-imperialism, identification of national interests with those of workers and peasants, and their association of sacrifice with social radicalism rather than religion have left behind an ideological legacy and organisational forms that have endured.

From the Jail Notebook

Theory of Divine Rights of Kings

[Patriarchal Theory]

In this very age when great many thinkers were thus propounding these principles of 'Sovereignty of the People', there were other theorists, who tried to prove that kingdom(s) being enlarged families, the patriarchal authority of the head of a household was transferred by primogenitary descent to the representative of the first sovereign who could be proved to have reigned over any nation.

Monarchy was therefore presumed to rest on an indefeasible right, and the king was held responsible to God alone! This was known as "Divine Rights of Kings!" This was known as the "Patriarchal Theory!"

Thomas Hobbes: In his various works written in 1642-1650-1651, he combined the doctrine of the unlimited authority of the sovereign, with the rival doctrine of an original compact of the people. Hobbes' defence of absolutism-passive obedience-was secular and rationalistic rather than theological. He regarded the happiness of the community (as a whole) as the great end of government.

Man an unsociable animal!

Perpetual danger forces them to form state!

Hobbes' philosophy is cynical. According to him a man's impulses are naturally directed to his own preservation and pleasure and he cannot aim at anything but their gratification. Therefore man is unsociable by nature! He says "in the natural state every man is at war with his fellows; and the life of everyone is in danger, solitary, poor, unsafe brutish and short."** It is the fear of this sort of life that impelled them to political union. Since mere pact wouldn't do, hence the establishment of 'supreme common power the govt.' 'Conquest' or 'acquisition' and 'institution' the only basis of all states

Society is founded by "acquisition" i.e. by conquest or "institution" viz. by mutual contract or compact. In the latter case once the sovereign authority is established all must obey. Anybody rebelling must perish. He should be destroyed.

Unlimited Authority of the Sovereign!

He gives the rights of Legislature, Judicature and Executive-one and all to the sovereign. To be effective, he writes, 'the sovereign power must be unlimited, irreclaimable and indivisible. Unlimited power may indeed give rise to mischief, but the worst of these is not so bad as civil war or anarchism.

In all likelihood, these are not quotations, but Bhagat Singh's own observations.

While the second part of the quote is from Leviathan, the first is Bhagat Singh's (or someone else's) paraphrasing. The Leviathan itself does not contain these words. Indeed, it is interesting that Hobbes hardly ever uses the terms 'natural state' or 'state of nature'.

H.S.R.A.: DECISIVE TURN TOWARDS SOCIALISM

After the British attempts to smash the HRA in the Kakori Conspiracy Case, the regrouping of the Kanpur group began under the leadership of Chandrashekhar Azad. He was assisted by Kundan Lal Gupta, Shiv Verma, Bejoy Kumar Sinha, Jaidev Kapur, Gaya Prasad and others. The Lahore group was led by Bhagat Singh and comprised Bhagwati Charan Vohra, Sukhdev, Kishori Lal, Yashpal and others.

The ideological churning within the HRA leadership continued unabated during this period. Shiv Verma has written that the credit for bringing Bhagat Singh and the Lahore group from anarchism to socialism goes to prominent Communist leader Sohan Singh Josh and to Lala Chhabil Das, who was the principal of the National College. The Dwarkadas Library of Lala Lajpat Rai, which had such books on Marxism and Soviet Russia that were not banned by the

British, and other illegal sources of Marxist literature, also played a crucial role in getting Bhagat Singh and Bhagwati Charan over to Marxism. The Kanpur group was similarly influenced by Radha Mohan Gokulji, Maulana Hasrat Mohani and Satyabhakta, who had declared themselves as Communists. Ganesh Shankar Vidyarthi also helped the young revolutionaries in many ways. As in Lahore, so also in Kanpur, legal and illegal Marxist literature also played a key role.

Added to this process of self-cultivation were also the political developments taking place in the country during this period. Some of these were: the five Peshawar Conspiracy Cases from 1922-27 that were instituted by the British against several muhajirs who came back from Soviet Russia and either were, or were suspected to be, Communists; the Kanpur Conspiracy Case of 1923-24 against Communist leaders; the first All-India conference of the CPI at Kanpur in December 1925; the formation of Workers' and Peasants' Parties in various provinces in 1926-28; the world economic crisis that began in the colonies from 1926; the historic general strike of the British working class in 1926; and the unprecedented strike struggles of the Indian working class led by the Communists in various parts of the country from 1926-28. All these developments could not have failed to make their impact on the young revolutionaries of the HRA.

It was against this background that a key meeting of leading revolutionaries was held at the Ferozshah Kotla Grounds in Delhi on September 8-9, 1928. A total of eight representatives attended the meeting. There were from two from Punjab, three from Uttar Pradesh, two from Bihar and one from Rajasthan. The Bengal group did not attend, but it later sent Jatin Das to Agra to train the others in manufacturing bombs.

Bhagat Singh placed the following main proposals before the meeting: (a) that the time had come to boldly declare Socialism as our ultimate goal, (b) that the name of the Party be changed accordingly to Hindustan Socialist Republican Association (HSRA) so that the people would know our ultimate aim, (c) that we should undertake only such actions which have direct relationship with the demands and sentiments of the people, and not fritter away our time and energy in killing petty police officials and informers, (d) that for funds we should lay our hands on government money and avoid actions on private houses, and (e) that the principle of collective leadership should be strictly observed. After a detailed two-day discussion on these proposals, they were adopted by a majority of six to two. The six who voted in favour were Bhagat Singh, Sukhdev, Shiv Verma, Bejoy Kumar Sinha, Jaidev Kapur and Surendra Pandey. Phanindranath Ghosh and Manmohan Banerjee, both from Bihar, and both of whom were later to turn approvers in the Second Lahore Conspiracy Case against Bhagat Singh and others, opposed the idea of socialism as well as the change in the name of the Party.

Chandrashekhar Azad did not attend the meeting for security reasons, but he had been fully consulted by Bhagat Singh, and had given his assent to the above proposals. The meeting elected a seven-member central committee. Bhagat Singh was given the charge of ideological work and Chandrashekhar Azad was elected commander-in-chief.

The HSRA Manifesto, written by Bhagwati Charan Vohra and widely distributed in the Lahore Session of the Congress in December 1929, is a remarkable document. Beginning with the sentence "The food on which the tender plant of liberty thrives is the blood of the martyr," the Manifesto lyrically explains the meaning of Revolution thus: "Revolution is a phenomenon which nature loves and without which there can be no progress either in nature or in human affairs.

Revolution is certainly not unthinking, brutal campaign of murder and incendiarism; it is not a few bombs thrown here and a few shots fired there; neither is it a movement to destroy all remnants of civilization and blow to pieces time honoured principles of justice and equity. Revolution is not a philosophy of despair or a creed of desperadoes. Revolution may be anti-God but is certainly not anti-Man. It is a vital, living force which is indicative of eternal conflict between the old and the new, between life and living death, between light and darkness. There is no concord, no symphony, no rhythm without revolution. 'The music of the spheres' of which poets have sung, would remain an unreality if a ceaseless revolution were to be eliminated from the space. Revolution is Law, Revolution is Order and Revolution is the Truth."

Analyzing the current situation, the Manifesto says, "India is writhing under the yoke of imperialism. Her teeming millions are today a helpless prey to poverty and ignorance. Foreign domination and economic exploitation have unmanned the vast majority of the people who constitute the workers and peasants of India. The position of the Indian proletariat is, today, extremely critical. It has a double danger to face. It has to bear the onslaught of foreign capitalism on one hand and the treacherous attack of Indian capital on the other. The latter is showing a progressive tendency to join hands with the former. The leaning of certain politicians in favour of dominion status shows clearly which way the wind blows. Indian capital is preparing to betray the masses into the hands of foreign capitalism and receive as a price of this betrayal, a little share in the government of the country. The hope of the proletariat is now centred on socialism which alone can lead to the establishment of complete independence and the removal of all social distinctions and privileges."

While this certainly marked a significant advance over earlier declarations of all armed freedom fighters so far, hangovers of the past legacy were not obliterated altogether. A certain amount of confusion still prevailed in the Manifesto about the role of terrorism. For instance, "We have been taken to task for our terroristic policy. Our answer is that terrorism is never the object of revolutionaries, nor do they believe that terrorism alone can bring independence. No doubt the revolutionaries think, and rightly, that it is only by resorting to terrorism alone that they can find a most effective means of retaliation. The British government exists, because the Britishers have been successful in terrorizing the whole of India. How are we to meet this official terrorism? Only counter-terrorism on the part of revolutionaries can checkmate effectively this bureaucratic bullying."

The other major document of the HSRA was called The Philosophy of the Bomb. It had an interesting background. On December 23, 1929, a bomb exploded under Viceroy Irwin's special train, from which he escaped death or serious injury. Gandhiji thanked

God for the Viceroy's narrow escape and in the Lahore session of the Congress that was held the very next week, Gandhiji wanted a resolution passed unanimously 'condemning the cowardly deed of the misguided youth.' But the Congress was in no mood to oblige, and the resolution was passed by a bare majority of 81 in a house of 1713.

After this, Gandhiji wrote a piece called The Cult of the Bomb in his journal Young India. To this, Bhagwati Charan Vohra, in full consultation with Chandrashekhar Azad, wrote a reply called The Philosophy of the Bomb. That was also published in Young India. It was an outstanding document, the most mature that the HSRA produced. It polemically countered Gandhiji's attack on the armed revolutionaries, criticized his creed of nonviolent satyagraha, reiterated the aim of a socialist revolution and ended with the stirring battle-cry:

"We take this opportunity to appeal to our countrymen-to the youth, to the workers and peasants, to the revolutionary intelligentsia-to come forward and join us in carrying aloft the banner of freedom. Let us establish a new order of society in which political and economic exploitation will be an impossibility...There is no crime that Britain has not committed in India. Deliberate misrule has reduced us to paupers, has 'bled us white'. As a race and a people we stand dishonoured and outraged. Do people still expect us to forget and to forgive? We shall have our revenge-a people's righteous revenge on the tyrant. Let the cowards fall back and cringe for compromise and peace. We ask for no mercy and we give no quarter. Ours is a war to the end-to Victory or Death. Long Live Revolution!"

THE ASSASSINATION OF SAUNDERS

In 1928, the all-white Simon Commission came to India to probe the question of further constitutional reforms. The Congress decided to boycott the Commission and to hold protest demonstrations against it. The HSRA decided to actively participate in these actions. The Commission came to Lahore on October 30, 1928, less than two months after the formation of the HSRA. A huge demonstration, led by Lala Lajpat Rai, was held. Bhagat Singh and his comrades were part of it. The police ordered a lathi charge and the Superintendent of Police named Scott rained lathi blows on Lajpat Rai's head. He died on November 17. The nation was stunned and infuriated.

The HSRA decided to avenge the death of Lajpat Rai and the insult to the nation by killing Scott. On December 17, 1928, exactly a month after Lajpat Rai's death, Bhagat Singh, Chandrashekhar Azad, Rajguru and Sukhdev shot dead J P Saunders, another police officer who was also involved in the lathi charge, mistaking him for Scott.

The same night, handwritten posters in pink were pasted on the walls of Lahore. Issued by the Hindustan Socialist Republican Army, which claimed responsibility for the killing, the powerful poster said: "With the death of J P Saunders, the assassination of Lala Lajpat Rai has been avenged...This national insult was a challenge to young men. Today the world has seen that the people of India are not lifeless; their blood has not become cold. They can lay down their lives for the country's honour. The proof of this has been given by the youth who are ridiculed and insulted by the leaders of their own country." The poster continued: "We are sorry to have killed a man. But this man was a part of a cruel, despicable and unjust system and killing him was a necessity. This man has been killed as an employee of the British government. This government is the most oppressive government in the world. We are sorry for shedding human blood but it becomes necessary to bathe the altar of revolution with blood. Our aim is to bring about a revolution which would end all exploitation of man by man. Long Live Revolution!"

After the assassination of Saunders, Bhagat Singh immediately escaped to Calcutta along with Rajguru and Bhagwati Charan's wife Durga Bhabhi, who was a dedicated revolutionary in her own right. All three were in disguise. In Calcutta, Bhagat Singh met the Bengal revolutionaries Trailokya Chakravarty and Pratul Ganguly who had by that time come out of jail. He reported to them about the HSRA decisions taken in the September meeting in Delhi and obtained their assent on all the points. They agreed to send Jatin Das to train the HSRA revolutionaries in manufacturing bombs.

Bhagat Singh attended in secret the first All India Conference of the Workers' and Peasants' Parties which was held at Calcutta from December 21-24, 1928. Sohan Singh Josh and others from Punjab attended the conference as delegates. Bhagat Singh was also present during the Calcutta session of the Congress which was held from December 29, 1928 to January 1, 1929. Here, on the first day, the Communist Party made a historic intervention when it led a huge demonstration of over 50,000 workers which occupied the Congress pandal and demanded that the Congress accept the goal of complete independence instead of dominion status at this session itself. That did not happen. This long-standing demand of the Indian people, which was first raised by the Communist Party, was finally accepted one year later, at the Lahore session of the Congress on December 31, 1929.

Shiv Verma has recalled an interesting and significant anecdote of that time. He writes: "While talking to Comrade Sohan Singh Josh at Calcutta in December 1928, at the time of the Calcutta session of the Congress, Bhagat Singh had said, 'We entirely agree with the programme and activities of your Party, but there are times when the blow of the enemy has to be immediately counteracted by armed actions to inspire confidence among the masses.' That is how our minds were working then."

For four months, from December 1928 to April 1929, the British regime, in spite of desperate efforts, could not trace those responsible for the assassination of Saunders. It was the next episode in the struggle that was to provide them with the clues.

Bombs in the Central Assembly

To crack down on the rising working class movement and the increasing influence of the Communists, the British government brought the repressive Public Safety Bill and the Trade Disputes Bill in the Central Legislative Assembly at Delhi. Already, on March 20, 1929, the British regime had arrested 31 prominent Communist and labour leaders from different parts of the country in the famous Meerut Conspiracy Case. The HSRA leadership decided to throw bombs in the Central Assembly to protest against the passage of the above two draconian Bills and also against the arrests of the Communist and labour leaders. The bombs were not meant to kill anybody; they were to serve as a warning. Those throwing the bombs would not escape, but would deliberately get arrested and then use the trial in court for propaganda so that the programme and ideology of the HSRA would become widely known throughout the country.

After considerable discussion, it was decided that Bhagat Singh and Batukeshwar Dutt should carry out this task. Bhagat Singh would put forth the views of the revolutionaries before the court and the country most effectively, and the presence of Batukeshwar Dutt would stress the All-India character of the HSRA. This decision was taken although it was fraught with grave risk, since Bhagat Singh was also involved in the Saunders case. On April 8, 1929, as planned, Bhagat Singh and Batukeshwar Dutt threw two bombs in the Assembly, immediately after the passage of the Trade Disputes Bill. No one was seriously injured. They also threw leaflets in the Assembly proclaiming why they had thrown the bombs. They did not try to run away and calmly courted arrest.

The leaflet thrown in the Assembly, in the name of the Hindustan Socialist Republican Association, began thus: "It takes a loud voice to make the deaf hear. With these immortal words uttered on a similar occasion by Valliant, a French anarchist martyr, do we strongly justify this action of ours...The Government is thrusting upon us new repressive measures like the Public Safety and the Trade Disputes Bill, while reserving the Press Sedition Bill for the next session.

The indiscriminate arrests of labour leaders working in the open field clearly indicate whither the wind blows..."

"Let the representatives of the people return to their constituencies and prepare the masses for the coming revolution, and let the Government know that while protesting against the Public Safety and Trade Disputes Bills and the callous murder of Lala Lajpat Rai, on behalf of the helpless Indian masses, we want to emphasize the lesson often repeated by history, that it is easy to kill individuals but you cannot kill the ideas. Great empires crumbled while the ideas survived. Bourbons and Czars fell.

"We are sorry to admit that we who attach so great a sanctity to human life, we who dream of a glorious future, when man will be enjoying perfect peace and full liberty, have been forced to shed human blood. But the sacrifice of individuals at the altar of the 'Great Revolution' that will bring freedom to all, rendering the exploitation of man by man impossible, is inevitable. Long Live Revolution! "

Both the above actions-the assassination of Saunders and the hurling of bombs in the Central Assembly-made Bhagat Singh and his comrades legendary heroes. The whole country acclaimed them with admiration and adulation. The acclamation was to increase even more after seeing their fearless defiance in British jails and before British courts.

AN INTELLECTUAL GIANT

By all accounts, Bhagat Singh was of a scholarly bent of mind and a deep thinker who understood the power of ideas. "The sword of revolution", he told the judges trying him, "is sharpened at the whetstone of thought". On being asked as to what set him apart from other revolutionaries, Shiv Verma, a fellow revolutionary and a close comrade-in-arms, replied thus: "I can tell you that in just one sentence: Bhagat Singh was our undisputed ideological leader. I do not remember a single moment when Bhagat Singh did not have a book in his pocket. The other virtues of Bhagat Singh like tremendous courage and so on were there in the other revolutionaries amongst us also. But his uniqueness lay in his great studiousness. The degree of clarity and integrity that he had about the aims of our movement, was not there in any of us at that time".

Well-known Indian historian Bipan Chandra has correctly observed that "Bhagat Singh was already at a young age a giant of an intellectual and thinker". Chaman Lall, who edited all of Bhagat Singh's manuscripts, noted that Bhagat Singh had command of four languages-Punjabi, Hindi, Urdu and English-without much formal training or education. He wrote in all these languages and his prison notebooks contain "... excerpts from 108 authors and 43 books including prominently Marx, Engels and Lenin, but also many others".

Bhagat Singh's quest for knowledge, his rigorous pursuit of a scientific under-pinning for his revolutionary beliefs and activity, becomes clear from the remarkable article, 'Why I am an Atheist', which he wrote shortly before his execution. In it, he explains that during the earlier period of his activity he had merely been a romantic revolutionary. Then came the time to shoulder the whole responsibility. It was a time when the very existence of the revolutionary movement appeared impossible-a time when not only "enthusiastic comrades", but even leaders began to "jeer at us". Continuing, Bhagat Singh, reveals the mental torture he went through in the following moving words:

> *"For some time I was afraid that some day I also might be convinced of the futility of our own programme. That was a turning point in my revolutionary career. 'Study' was the cry that reverberated in the corridors of my mind. Study to enable yourself to face the arguments advanced by opposition. Study to arm yourself with arguments in favour of your cult. I began to study. My previous faith and convictions underwent a remarkable modification. The romance of the violent methods alone which was so prominent amongst our predecessors was replaced by serious ideas. No more mysticism, no more blind faith. Realism became our cult. Use of force justifiable when resorted to as a matter of terrible necessity: nonviolence as policy indispensable for all mass movement. So much about methods. The most important thing was the clear conception of the ideal for which we were to fight. As there were no important activities in the field of action I got ample opportunity to study various ideals of the world revolution. I studied Bakunin, the Anarchist leader, something of Marx the father of Communism and much of Lenin, Trotsky and others, the men who had successfully carried out a revolution in their country".*

What is more, Bhagat Singh was born at a time of the rising tide of the anti-colonial movement and widespread discontent. Alarmed by the mood of the people, Denzil Ibbetson, the Lieutenant Governor, noted in a report: "Everywhere people are sensible of a change, of a 'new air' ..., which is blowing through men's minds, and are waiting to see what will come of it. ... In the towns of Rawalpindi, Sialkot and Lyallpur, active anti-English propaganda is being openly and sedulously preached. In Lahore, the capital of the province, the propaganda is virulent and has resulted in a more or less general state of serious unrest" (quoted in K.K.Khullar, Shaheed Bhagat Singh, pp.98-110).

Far from subsiding, the wave of anti-colonial feelings and agitation gained increasing strength in the years following 1907. Growing up in this milieu, brought up on stories of the exploits of his uncle and father, Bhagat Singh could hardly have failed to imbibe patriotic and anti-colonial sentiments. He was only eight when Punjab was plunged into turmoil following the hanging of Seven Ghadar revolutionaries by the British colonial authorities on 16-17 November 1915 in the First Lahore Conspiracy Case. One of those hanged was Kastar Singh Sarabha, who was only 19 at the time of his judicial murder by the British. Sarabha's last words were: "My only ambition is to see my country free. All that I did had this objective. I have never done anything out of hatred for any person, nation, religion or race. I only desire one thing-independence. This is my only dream. If I had to live more lives than one, I would sacrifice each of them for my country's sake".

Sarabha became Bhagat Singh's hero, whose photo Bhagat Singh always carried in his pocket and was carrying at the time of his arrest in 1929. When in 1926, Bhagat Singh, along with Sukhdev and Bhagwati Charan Vohra (BCV) founded the Naujawan Bharat Sabha in Lahore, its inaugural meeting was preceded by the unveiling of Sarabha's portrait in daring and open defiance of the colonial authorities.

The Ghadar Party (party of revolt) was formed on 21 April 1913 by Indian revolutionaries then resident in Canada and the USA. The formation of the Ghadar marked the beginning of the latest and most modern phase of India's freedom movement; with its formation, the revolutionary movement in India took a giant step forward. In its outlook the Ghadar Party was internationalist and secular; it stressed the importance of revolutionary work in the army with the aim of inciting the latter to rise in rebellion against the British imperialist rule; it drew its ranks from the peasants turned factory workers, unlike earlier revolutionaries who had by and large hailed from the lower middle-class intelligentsia.

The Ghadar movement, though cruelly suppressed by the British imperial authorities, left a rich revolutionary legacy and made an indelible mark on the freedom movement, inspiring in the process an entire generation of revolutionaries with its courage, outlook and death-defying heroism.

Just over three years after the martyrdom of the leaders of the Ghadar movement came the Amritsar (Jallianwala) massacre, which claimed the lives of over a thousand innocent men, women and children, and left many more wounded. This senseless massacre on the orders of the butcher of Amritsar, General Dyer, on 13 April 1919, left a lasting impression on Bhagat Singh, who was just twelve year old then.

According to records, enraged by the dastardly deed of the colonial government, Bhagat Singh went straight from his school to Amritsar, kissed the earth sanctified by the blood of Dyer's victims, and brought back with him a little of the blood-soaked soil which he kept in a bottle as a permanent reminder of the injustice, injury and humiliation perpetrated by the colonial rulers on the Indian people.

Bhagat Singh and his comrades were not the first fighters against British colonialism; nor were they the first to take up arms against the British Raj. What distinguished them from the several thousands of armed fighters for Indian freedom over a period of nearly two centuries is, first, that the revolutionary activities of Bhagat Singh and his comrades happened to coincide with the tumultuous arrival of the Indian masses into the arena of political life and, second, that they were irresistibly driven to accept the ideology of Marxism.

October Revolution

In this regard, the Great October Socialist Revolution in Russia played a most crucial role. Such was the liberating effect of the

Russian Revolution that even some Congress leaders, such as Bal Gangadhar Tilka, Lala Lajpat Rai and Bipin Chandra Pal, greeted with joy the Bolshevik victory and the Bolshevik programme.

The Russian Revolution, by laying bare the contrast between the compromising bourgeois Congress leadership of the Indian freedom struggle, on the one hand, and the uncompromising revolutionary Bolshevik leadership, on the other, had an even bigger impact on the young armed freedom fighters in India and elsewhere.

The October Revolution, with its earth-shattering ramifications, had a triple effect on the young Indian revolutionaries in particular. First, it instilled confidence in them that imperialism and the system of exploitation of one man by another, and one nation by another, could be got rid of. Second, it forced them to seriously ponder the meaning-the economic and social content-of independence.

Third, it prompted a serious study of Marxism as the only reliable weapon and ideological tool for the attainment of the freedom of the Indian people from British colonialism and the system of exploitation alike.

Bhagat Singh in particular was deeply influenced by the triumphant march of the October Revolution. Less than two months before his execution, in what can only be called his last testament, this is how he exposes, by an implicit reference to the events of the 1920s, the compromising capitulationist and cowardly leadership of the Congress, above all Gandhi, as the enemy of the Indian proletariat and peasantry and a friend of the exploiting bourgeois and landlord classes:

"The real revolutionary armies are in the villages and in factories, the peasantry and the labourers. But our bourgeois leaders do not and cannot dare to tackle them. The sleeping lion once awakened from its slumber shall become irresistible even after the achievement of what our leaders aim at. After his first experience with the Ahmedabad labourers in 1920 Mahatma Gandhi declared: 'We must not tamper with the labourers. It is dangerous to make political use of the factory proletariat' (The Times, May 1921). Since then, they never dared to approach them. There remains the peasantry. The

Bardoli resolution of 1922 clearly defines the horrors the leaders felt when they saw the gigantic peasant class rising to shake off not only the domination of an alien nation but also the yoke of the landlords. It is there that our leaders prefer surrender to the British than to the peasantry".

It was also in the aftermath of the October Revolution, and under its direct impact, that the Communist Party of India was formed at Tashkent on 17 October 1920, and the All India Trade Union Congress (AITUC) established on 31 October 1920 in Bombay. Both these bodies were to play an important role in the anti-colonial and revolutionary movement.

Kakori Trial

In 1924, still in his teens, Bhagat Singh left Lahore for Kanpur, where he completed his study of Marx's Capital, met many revolutionaries, including Batukeshwar Dutt, who taught him Bengali, and Chandrashekar Azad, and joined the Hindustan Republican Association (HRA), which had been formed in 1923, with Sachindra Nath Sanyal being it moving spirit. The object clause of the HRA's Rules and Regulations stated: "The object of the Association shall be to establish a Federal Republic of the United States of India by an armed revolution". It was to be a republic in which exploitation of one person by another would be outlawed.

The HRA was to be "not national but international" in its outlook and follow in the footsteps of "Bolshevik Russia". Funds for the HRA were to be raised, among other things, through armed robberies. It was to this end that the HRA revolutionaries stopped a train on 9 August 1925 at Kakori near Lucknow, looted a government safe containing the modest sum of Rs4,679, in the process killing one person accidentally.

Most of the participants in the train robbery were arrested and tried in the Kakori Conspiracy Case. Four of the accused in this case, including the famous poet Ram Prasad Bismil, were hanged, two received life imprisonment and eleven others varying prison terms. Only two, including the legendary Chandrashekar Azad, managed to evade arrest. Although a heavy blow to the HRA, the Kakori case acquired the proportions of a legend in view of the display of courage and manhood by the accused during the trial. The four sentenced to be hanged cheerfully mounted the gallows while singing the following legendary song, which was from then on to be on the lips of literally every Indian:

"Sarfaroshi ki tamanna ab hamare dil mein hai,

"Dekhna hai zor kitna basu-e katil mein hai".

"We are burning with a longing to be denuded of our heads,

"We shall see how much strength can the executioner's arms wield".

Thanks to the strenuous work of Azad and the second line of leadership, which included Shiv Verma and many others, the HRA was able to recover from the setback following the Kakori Conspiracy Case.

Naujawan Bharat Sabha (NBS)

Meanwhile, after a six-month stay in Kanpur, Bhagat Singh returned to Lahore. He had only gone to Kanpur to escape pressure from his father and grandmother to get married. His correspondence with his father on this question clearly brings out Bhagat Singh's lofty ideals in the service of which he was ready to renounce all worldly comforts and sacrifice his life. "Now is not the time for marriage. The country is calling me. I have taken oath to serve the country physically, mentally and monetarily", he wrote to his father. Alluding to his family's patriotism and its sacrifices in the service of the freedom struggle, he continued "I am only following your footprints ... you will kindly not tie me in matrimony but give me your blessings so that I may succeed in my mission". In response to a letter from his father saying that "We have already settled your marriage ... you should not create any difficulty", Bhagat Singh wrote a firm, but respectful reply. "I am astonished to read the contents of your letter. When you, who are a staunch patriot and brave personality, can be influenced by such trifles, then what will happen to ordinary men?

"You are caring for Dadi [my grandmother], but in how much trouble is our Mother of 33 crores [330 million], the Bharat Mata

[Mother India]. We will have to sacrifice everything for her sake". At the time of leaving for Kanpur, he left this note: "Revered Father, ... I have dedicated my life to the lofty goal of service to the Motherland. Hence there is no attraction in me for home and fulfilment of worldly desires. ... I hope you will forgive me".

Six months later, when assured that his father would no longer insist on him getting married, Bhagat Singh returned to Lahore, only more ardent than ever before, to continue along a path in the service of which he had dedicated his life. While remaining in touch with his fellow revolutionaries in the United Provinces (UP) after his return to Lahore, Bhagat Singh extended and deepened his contacts in Punjab. In March 1926, along with Sukhdev, B.C.Vohra and Ram Krishan, he formed the Naujawan Bharat Sabha (NBS) [Indian Youth Association], which took up the unrealised mission of the HRA. In addition to the youth, the NBS's membership included such eminent people as Saifuddin Kitchlew, Satyapal, Mir Abdul Majid, Sardul Singh Caveeshar and the poet Lal Chand Falaq. Ram Krishan was the NBS's President and Bhagat Singh, its Secretary.

The progress of the NBS was truly phenomenal. Its branches spread throughout the Punjab, and similar organisations were set up in other provinces. An All-India NBS was established in Delhi, which soon thereafter forged links with the HRA and the Kirti Kisan [Workers and Peasants] Party founded by the veteran communist leader Sohan Singh Josh. The NBS was to function openly as a legal arm of the revolutionary movement and undertake political work in the ranks of the youth as well as among workers and peasants. As such, recognising as it did the importance of political work among the broad masses of people, the NBS, its aims and programme, marked a very important step forward in the political and ideological development of Bhagat Singh and his close comrades and the acceptance by them of Marxist methods of work as well as Marxist ideology.

The political aims of the NBS included, inter alia, the establishment of a completely independent workers' and peasants' republic in India; the organisation of labourers and peasants; instilling the sprit of patriotism in the country's youth; and fighting against communalism (the pitting of one religious group against another). "Revolution by the masses and for the masses" was the motto of the NBS's Manifesto, written by B.C.Vohra. The masses must be made to realise, said the Manifesto, that "... the revolution which is to come will mean more than a change of masters. It will, above all, mean the birth of a new order of things, a new state", requiring decades of "matchless self-sacrifice", adding that a "... revolutionary does not necessarily mean a man of bombs and revolvers".

The rules of the NBS were written by Bhagat Singh. Such was the importance attached by Bhagat Singh to the need for fighting the corrosive disease of communalism that two out of its six rules called for the creation of "... the spirit of general toleration among the public concerning religion as a matter of personal belief of man", and to "... have nothing to do with communal bodies or other parties which disseminate communal ideas". Believing religion to be the private concern of an individual, Bhagat Singh was firmly of the view that the moment it intruded into politics and donned the garb of communalism, religion had to be fought like an enemy. He was of the view that communalism was no less an enemy than colonialism. More than any other contemporary leader, Bhagat Singh worked tirelessly to free the masses from the servitude of religion and superstition. As is clear from his wonderful article 'Why I am an Atheist', he rightly poured scorn and ridicule on the concept of a world created by a supreme being.

So strong was Bhagat Singh's hatred of communalism that he went to the extent of publicly denouncing, though without naming him, the eminent Congress leader in Punjab, Lal Lajpat Rai, for avenging whose death at the hands of British colonialism he was to pay for with his own life. As Lajpat Rai's politics took a markedly communal turn in the mid-twenties, Bhagat Singh printed, as a pamphlet, Robert Browning's famous poem, 'The Lost Leader', in which Browning subjected Wordsworth to trenchant criticism for his renegacy against the French Revolution and the spirit of liberty. In the words of Dr. Bipin Chandra: "... The opening line of the poem was 'Just for a handful of silver he left us;, a few other lines were

'We shall march prospering-not thro' his presence; songs may inspire us-from his lyre'; and 'Blot out his name, record one lost soul'-in fact, his name appeared nowhere in it-only the front cover carried Lajpat Rai's photograph".

In 1928 Bhagat Singh successfully argued that young persons belonging to religious-communal organisations be barred from the membership of the NBS.

From HRA to HSRA

In the aftermath of the Kakori trial, which was intended by the colonial authorities to smash the Hindustan Republican Association (HRA), the latter began regrouping under the leadership of Azad. At the same time, global and national political and economic developments were increasingly pushing the HRA revolutionaries in the direction of Marxism. In their never-ceasing thirst for knowledge, the HRA revolutionaries, especially Bhagat Singh, devoured voluminous amounts of literature, including Marxist literature.

Their enlightenment through literature was supplemented by lessons driven home by the various conspiracy cases, especially the Kanpur Conspiracy Trial of 1923-24 against the communists, the world economic crisis which made its appearance in the colonies as early as 1926, the historic British General Strike of 1926, and a wave of unprecedented and momentous strikes of the Indian proletariat under communist leadership in several parts of the country.

These developments left their stamp on the HRA revolutionaries and furnish the background to the crucial meeting of the HRA held at Ferozeshah Kotla ground in Delhi on 8-9 September 1928. Present at this meeting were representatives from Punjab, UP, Bihar and Rajasthan.

The Punjab group was led by Bhagat Singh, who played a leading role. He put forward at this meeting the following major proposals: First, that socialism be accepted as the ultimate goal of the organisation; second, that consequently the name of the party, in order to reflect the goal of socialism, be changed to Hindustan Socialist Republican Association (HSRA); third, that only such actions be undertaken by the party as those bearing a direct relationship with the desires, demands and interests of the people, so as not to waste time and effort in killing petty police functionaries and informers; fourth, that the principle of collective leadership be accepted as the basis of the party's functioning and be strictly adhered to; and, finally, that for securing funds, the target should be government resources and not private houses. These proposals were accepted by a majority of six against two (the two dissidents-Phanindranath Ghosh and Manmohan Bannerjee-were to turn approvers in the Second Lahore Conspiracy Case against Bhagat Singh and others) and the meeting elected a seven-member Central Committee. Bhagat Singh was made responsible for ideological work and Azad was elected to be the Commander-in-chief of the HSRA.

The Manifesto of the HSRA, drafted by B.C.Vohra, is an extraordinary panegyric in praise of revolution-almost lyrical in form, powerful in its content and uplifting in its effect. Having stated that without revolution "... there can be no progress in nature or in human affairs", it carries on thus:

> *"Revolution is certainly not unthinking, brutal campaign of murder and incendiarism; it is not a few bombs thrown here and a few shots fired there; neither is it a movement to destroy all remnants of civilization and blow to pieces time honoured principles of justice and equity. Revolution is not a philosophy of despair or a creed of desperadoes. Revolution may be anti-God but is certainly not anti-Man. It is a vital, living force which is indicative of eternal conflict between the old and the new, between life and living death, between light and darkness. There is no concord, no symphony, no rhythm without revolution. 'The music of the spheres' of which poets have sung, would remain an unreality if a ceaseless revolution were to be eliminated from the space. Revolution is Law, Revolution is Order and Revolution is Truth".*

The Manifesto goes on to portray the miserable lot of the Indian masses, who suffered the double yoke of foreign capitalism as well as the attack of Indian capital. It laid bare the capitulatory and cowardly role played by the Indian capitalist class and its political representatives, warning the Indian masses against their treachery and bringing home to them the truth that their only hope lay in socialism, which alone could accomplish the establishment of true independence and remove all social distinctions and privileges.

"India", says the Manifesto, "is writhing under the yoke of imperialism. Her teeming millions are today a helpless prey to poverty and ignorance. Foreign domination and economic exploitation have unmanned the vast majority of the people who constitute the workers and peasants of India. The position of the Indian proletariat is, today, extremely critical. It has a double danger to face. It has to bear the onslaught of foreign capitalism on one hand the treacherous attack of Indian capital on the other. The latter is showing a progressive tendency to join hands with the former. The leaning of certain politicians in favour of dominion status shows clearly which way the wind blows. Indian capital is preparing to betray the masses into the hands of foreign capitalism and receive as a price of this betrayal, a little share in the government of the country. The hope of the proletariat is now centred on socialism which alone can lead to the establishment of complete independence and the removal of all social distinctions and privileges".

Role of Revolutionary Terror

While emphasising the need for mobilising the broad masses in their fight against colonial bondage and class oppression and exploitation, the Manifesto correctly goes on to stress the need for, and the place of, armed revolutionary struggle in pursuit of the ideals of freedom and emancipation. It says:

> *"We have been taken to task for our terroristic policy. Our answer is that terrorism is never the object of revolutionaries, nor do they believe that terrorism alone can bring independence. No doubt the revolutionaries think, and rightly, that it is only by resorting to terrorism alone that they can find a most effective means of retaliation. The British government exists because the Britishers have been*

successful in terrorizing the whole of India. How are we to meet this official terrorism? Only counter-terrorism on the part of revolutionaries can checkmate effectively this bureaucratic bullying".

Certain writers, even some who call themselves communist, have put on record their disapproval of the lines quoted immediately above, allegedly betraying the partiality of Bhagat Singh and his comrades to terrorist methods of struggle. Only by misunderstanding, or worse, deliberately distorting, the meaning of these lines and dogmatically objecting to the use of the words 'terror' and 'terrorism' can one criticise their authors as being trigger happy terrorists. In our view, these lines express no more than that counter-revolutionary terror can only be answered by revolutionary terror. And of this, Bhagat Singh and his comrades were fully, and rightly, convinced. It would not be difficult to cite many examples of similar expressions of thought, and similar use of language, from the writing of V.I.Lenin, against whom it would occur to no one to level the accusation of terrorism.

The attempt to smear Bhagat Singh and his comrades by sticking on them the label of terrorism bears an uncanny resemblance to the shameful characterisation of the 1916 Easter uprising in Ireland, not only by the imperialist bourgeoisie but also by the overwhelming majority of the working-class parties of Europe at the time, as a mere putsch. No less a person than V.I.Lenin poured derision on such a "monstrously doctrinaire and pedantic opinion". "The term putsch", he said, "in its scientific sense, may be employed when the attempt at insurrection has revealed nothing but a circle of conspirators or stupid maniacs, and has aroused no sympathy among the masses". This, he went on, was not the case insofar as the Irish rebellion was concerned, for the centuries-old Irish liberation movement, "having passed through various stages and combinations, expressed itself, among other things, in a mass Irish National Congress in America, which called for Irish independence; it also expressed itself in street fighting conducted by a section of the urban petty bourgeoisie and a section of the workers after a long period of mass agitation, demonstrations, suppression of papers, etc. Whoever calls such a rebellion a 'putsch' is either a hardened reactionary, or a doctrinaire who is hopelessly incapable of envisaging a social revolution as a living phenomenon."

Without in the least impugning the strength and vitality of the Irish liberation movement in 1916, one can confidently say that the anti-imperialist and anti-colonialist struggle of the Indian people during the time that Bhagat Singh and his comrades were carrying out their revolutionary activities had developed to an incomparably higher level-Bhagat Singh and his comrades were inseparably connected with, and an extension of, the powerful national movement of the Indian people, which was shaking the very foundations of British rule in India. Far from revealing them to be "... a circle of conspirators or stupid maniacs", their actions aroused mass sympathy among the Indian masses, who took up the cause and slogans of these revolutionary heroes as their own and, who through their love and adoration for the self-sacrificing heroism of the revolutionaries in the cause of the emancipation of the Indian masses, turned them into living legends. Only those who are hardened reactionaries, "hopelessly incapable of envisaging a socialist revolution as a living phenomenon" can condemn them as terrorists. In fact such was the popular acclaim for the courageous acts of Bhagat Singh and his comrades that even a hardened reactionary like Gandhi who, as we shall reveal later on, played such a dirty and complicity role in the judicial murder of these brave and wonderful sons of India, was obliged, under mass pressure, to shower praise on them-no matter how grudgingly and meanly.

Even today, seventy six years after their martyrdom, there are some who continue to accuse Bhagat Singh and his comrades of being infatuated with the ideology of anarchistic terrorism, in isolation from the masses. This, notwithstanding clear statements to the contrary by Bhagat Singh such as these, in which, while emphasising the significance and role of revolutionary violence, he forswears the use of terrorism as a method of struggle:

> *"Apparently I have acted like a terrorist. But I am not a terrorist. I am a revolutionary who has got definite ideas of a lengthy programme as is being discussed here ... Let me announce with all the strength at my command, that I am*

not a terrorist and I never was, except perhaps in the beginning of my revolutionary career. And I am convinced that we cannot get anything through these methods. ... I do not mean that bombs and pistols are useless, rather the contrary. But I mean to say that mere bomb-throwing is not only useless, but sometimes harmful. The military department of the Party should always keep ready all the war material at its command for any emergency. It should back the political work of the Party. It cannot and should not act independently".

In a message from his prison cell, this is how Bhagat Singh laid stress on the seizure of state power as an instrument for uprooting the existing social order based on exploitation:

"We mean by revolution the uprooting of the present social order. For this capture of state power is necessary. The state apparatus is now in the hands of the privileged class. The protection of the interests of the masses, the translation of our ideal into reality, that is, laying the foundation of society in accordance with the principles of Karl Marx, demand our seizure of this apparatus" (October 1930).

On 2 February 1931, less than two months before his judicial murder, Bhagat Singh wrote his memorable appeal 'To Young Political Workers', which has justly been deemed as his last testament. Having analysed the then prevailing political and social conditions and the cowardly and capitulatory programme and tactics of the Congress Party, he exhorted the youth to embrace the ideology of Marxism, join the Communist Party, work among the people and do everything in their power to organise the working class and the peasantry, and went on to lay before it (the youth) the following Leninist programme on maters of organisation:

"We require-to use the term so dear to Lenin-the 'professional revolutionaries'. The whole time workers who have no other ambition or life-work except the revolution. The greater the number of such workers organized into the Party, the greater the chances of your success. ... The name of the Party

should be the Communist Party. This Party of political workers, bound by strict discipline, should handle all other movements. It shall have to organize the peasants' and workers' parties, labour unions, and may even venture to capture the Congress and kindred political bodies. And in order to create political consciousness, not only of national politics but class politics as well, the Party should organize a big publishing campaign".

In 1928, the British government sent the Simon Commission to India to look into the question of further constitutional reforms-a mere hoax to delay India's independence. Indians had neither been consulted over the constitution and the remit of this mockery of a Commission, nor did India have any representation on it. In the circumstances the Congress leadership decided to boycott the Commission and stage protest demonstrations against it. The revolutionaries of the HSRA resolved to actively support the boycott and the demonstrations. On the occasion of the arrival of the Commission in Lahore on 30 October 1928, hardly two months after the formation of the HSRA, a mammoth protest demonstration was held under the leadership of Lala Lajpat Rai.

The police subjected the participants to a baton charge. During this brutal action, Lala Lajpat Rai received several blows on his head from a baton wielded by a superintendent of police by the name of Scott. Lajpat Rai died on 17 November 1928 from his injuries. The entire country was astounded, with everyone feeling the pain and humiliation resulting from the brutal and senseless murder of Lajpat Rai by the colonial authorities. The youth of the country were particularly infuriated and burned with a desire to avenge Lajpat Rai's murder.

It was in these circumstances that the HSRA decided to kill Scott. One month to the day after Lajpat Rai's death, on 17 December 1928, Bhagat Singh, Rajguru, Sukhdev and Chandrashekar Azad shot dead another police officer, J.P.Saunders, who too had taken part in the attack on the demonstration of 30 October, mistakenly believing him to be Scott. Handwritten bills pasted on the walls of Lahore the same night, in which the HSRA claimed responsibility for the killing of Saunders, stated, inter alia: "With the death of J.P.Saunders, the assassination of Lala Lajpat Rai has been avenged. ... This national insult was a challenge to young men. Today the world has seen that the people of India are not lifeless; their blood has not become cold. They can lay down their lives for the country's honour. The proof of this has been given by the youth who are ridiculed and insulted by the leaders of their own country".

Continues the HSRA statement: "We are sorry to have killed a man. But this man was a part of a cruel, despicable and unjust system and killing him was a necessity. This man has been killed as an employee of the British Government. This government is the most oppressive government in the world.

"We are sorry for shedding human blood but it becomes necessary to bathe the altar of revolution with blood. Our aim is to bring about a revolution which would end all exploitation of man by man.

"Long Live Revolution!"

For nearly four months, all the efforts of the colonial authorities in tracing those who killed Saunders proved utterly fruitless. Only the next episode in the revolutionary struggle provided them with the clues that led to Bhagat Singh and his comrades, their trial by a specially constituted tribunal and their judicial murder by the colonial authorities. Let us turn to this episode.

The colonial government had introduced the draconian Public Safety Bill and the Trade Disputes Bill in the Central Legislative Assembly at Delhi, with the twin aims of suppressing the vibrant rising working-class movement and checking the increasing influence of the communists within this movement. As a prelude to this, on 20 March 1929, the colonial regime had arrested 31 prominent labour and communist leaders in various parts of India and brought them to court to face conspiracy charges in the notorious Meerut Conspiracy Case.

The HSRA resolved to dramatically interrupt the proceedings of the Assembly by lobbing bombs into the Chamber for the sole purpose of registering a protest against the passage of the above-mentioned Bills and the arbitrary and unjust incarceration of the communist and labour leaders. Never meant to kill anyone, the bombs were merely to serve as a warning to the authorities. Those given the responsibility to throw the bombs were to make no attempt to escape; instead they were to court arrest and use the inevitable court trial for propagating and popularising the programme and ideology of the HSRA among the wider masses of India.

After long discussion, the task of throwing the bombs was assigned to Bhagat Singh and Batukeshwar Dutt. While the former, as its most ideologically equipped member, was to explain the views and programme of the HSRA before the court and, through it, to the wider masses, Batukeshwar was included to emphasise the national, all-India, character of the revolutionary organisation.

The inclusion of Bhagat Singh was fraught with extreme risk as he had been a participant in the killing of J.P.Saunders. Be that as it may, as per the decision of the HSRA, on 8 April 1929, Bhagat Singh and Batukeshwar Dutt threw two bombs in the Central Assembly Hall, immediately following the passage of the Trade Disputes Bill.

Hardly anyone was seriously injured. All the same, pandemonium broke out on the official benches. Bhagat Singh also fired two unaimed shots from a pistol. Bhagat Singh and Dutt began shouting their favourite slogans: "Inquilab Zindabad" and "Down with British Imperialism" and threw copies of a leaflet into the Assembly Chamber.

This leaflet, under the name of the HSRA, together with the joint statement of Bhagat Singh and Dutt (whose author was Bhagat Singh alone), read out on their behalf by their lawyer Asaf Ali on 6 June 1929 in Sessions Court, gives us an accurate picture of the motive and extent of intention of the HSRA in executing the Assembly bomb plan, as well as its views on the significance of the use of force in pursuit of revolutionary goals, and the meaning and content of the word 'Revolution' as understood by Bhagat Singh and his comrades.

It is well worth our while quoting extensively from these two documents and, in view of their significance, hopefully the reader will forgive us the use of lengthy quotations.

The leaflet thrown in the Assembly boldly announces that "It takes a loud voice to make the deaf hear...", adding that ".. while the people are expecting some more crumbs of reforms from the Simon Commission, ... the Government is thrusting upon them new repressive measures like the Public Safety and the Trade Disputes Bill, ... reserving the Press Sedition Bill for the next session. The indiscriminate arrests of labour leaders working in the open field clearly indicate wither the wind blows". It was these provocative conditions which had forced the HSRA to instruct its army to undertake the action it had, emphasising that while the government might succeed in killing a few individuals it will never succeed in stamping out the ideas concerning the liberation of the masses. Let the leaflet speak for itself:

"In these extremely provocative circumstances, the Hindustan Socialist Republican Association, in all seriousness, realizing their full responsibility, had decided and ordered its army to do this particular action, so that a stop be put to this humiliating farce and to let the alien bureaucratic exploiters do what they wish, but they must be made to come before the public eee in their naked form.

"Let the representatives of the people return to their constituencies and prepare the masses for the coming revolution, and let the Government know that while protesting against the Public Safety and Trade Disputes Bills and the callous murder of Lala Lajpat Rai, on behalf of the helpless Indian masses, we want to emphasize the lesson often repeated by history, that it is easy to kill individuals but you cannot kill the ideas. Great empires crumbled while the ideas survived. Bourbons and Czars fell.

"We are sorry to admit that we who attach so great a sanctity to human life, we who dream of a glorious future, when man will be enjoying perfect peace and full liberty, have been forced to shed human blood. But the sacrifice of individuals at the altar of the 'Great Revolution' that will bring freedom to all, rendering the exploitation of man by man impossible, is inevitable.

"Long Live the Revolution".

The 6 June statement of the accused in the court of judge Leonard Middleton, methodically and scientifically answers the charges laid against Bhagat Singh and Dutt, while throwing great light on their motivation and ideals. The question was raised in the court: Were bombs thrown into the Assembly Chamber and Why? To the first half of the question, the accused replied in the affirmative. As to the second half of the question, the accused found it necessary "to go into some detail to offer a full and frank explanation of [their] motive and the circumstances leading up to what has become a historic moment.

"When we are told by some of the police officers, who visited us in jail that Lord Irwin in his address to the joint session of the two houses described the event as an attack directed against no individual but against an institution itself, we readily recognised that the true significance of the incident had been correctly appreciated.

"We are next to none in our love for humanity. Far from having any malice against any individual, we hold human life sacred beyond words.

"We are neither perpetrators of dastardly outrages, and, therefore, a disgrace to the country, as the pseudo-socialist Dewan Chaman Lal is reported to have described us, nor are we 'Lunatics' as 'The Tribune' of Lahore and some others would have it believed".

The statement goes on to say that the action of the revolutionaries was a "... practical protest against the institution, which, since its birth, has eminently helped to display not only its worthlessness but its far-reaching power for mischief", an institution which existed only "to demonstrate to the world India's humiliation and helplessness", and which symbolised "... the overriding domination of an irresponsible and autocratic rule". While resolutions such as those concerning the repeal of the repressive and arbitrary measures, passed the by House were routinely and "contemptuously trampled under foot on the floor of the so-called Indian Parliament", the government proposals, "rejected as unacceptable by the elected members of the legislatures, have been restored by a mere stroke of the pen".

Continues the statement: "In short, we have utterly failed to find any justification for the existence of an institution which, despite all its pomp and splendour, organized with the hard earned money of the sweating millions of India, is only a hollow show and a mischievous make-believe. Alike, have we failed to comprehend the mentality of the public leaders who help the Government to squander public time and money on such a manifestly stage-managed exhibition of India's helpless subjection.

> *"We have been ruminating upon all these matters, as also upon the wholesale arrests of the leaders of the labour movement. When the introduction of the Trade Disputes Bill brought us into the Assembly to watch its progress, the course of the debate only served to confirm our conviction that the labouring millions of India had nothing to expect from an institution that stood as a menacing monument to the strangling of the exploiters and the serfdom of the helpless labourers.*
>
> *"Finally, the insult of what we consider, an inhuman and barbarous measure was hurled on the devoted head of the representatives of the entire country, and the starving and struggling millions were deprived of their primary right and the sole means of improving their economic welfare. None who has felt like us for the dumb driven drudges of labourers could possibly witness this spectacle with equanimity. None whose heart bleeds for them, who have given their life-blood in silence to the building up of the economic structure could repress the cry which this ruthless blow had wrung out of our hearts."*

In view of the above circumstance, the bomb had been dropped on the floor of the Assembly Chamber "... to register our protest on behalf of those who had no other means left to give expression to their heart-rending agony. Our purpose was 'to make the deaf hear' and to give the heedless a timely warning". That "... from under the seeming stillness of the sea of Indian humanity, a veritable storm is about to break out. We have only hoisted the 'danger-signal' to warn those who are speeding along without heeding the grave danger ahead ... " Taking a swipe at the apostles of Gandhian nonviolence, the statement says: "We have only marked the end of an era of utopian nonviolence, of whose futility the rising generation has been convinced beyond the shadow of doubt".

By way of an explanation on this question, the statement adds: " ... Force when aggressively applied is 'violence' and is, therefore, morally unjustifiable, but when it is used in furtherance of a legitimate cause, it has its moral justification. The elimination of force at all costs is utopian. ..."

6

Revolutionary Movement for Indian Independence

The Revolutionary movement for Indian Independence is a part of the comprising the actions of the underground revolutionary factions. Groups believing in armed revolution against the ruling British fall into this category, as opposed to the generally peaceful civil disobedience movement spearheaded by Mohandas Karamchand Gandhi. The revolutionary groups were mainly concentrated in Bengal, Maharashtra, Bihar, the United Provinces and Punjab. More groups were scattered across India.

Andhra Pradesh

Uyyalawada Narasimha Reddy (died 22 February 1847) was the son of a former Indian Telugu Polygar who was at the heart of a rebellion in 1846, where 5000 peasants rose up against the British East India Company (EIC) in Kurnool district, Rayalaseema Region of Andhra Pradesh. They were protesting changes to the traditional agrarian system introduced by the British in the first half of the nineteenth century. Those changes, which included the introduction of the ryotwari system and other attempts to maximize revenue impacted lower-status cultivators by depleting their crops and leaving them impoverished.

2019 Telugu Movie Sye Raa Narasimha Reddy is based on the life of Narasimha Reddy, portrayed by Legendary Actor Chiranjeevi

Beginnings

Apart from a few stray incidents, the armed rebellion against the British rulers was not organised before the beginning of the 20th century. The revolutionary philosophies and movement made its presence felt during the 1905 Partition of Bengal. Arguably, the initial steps to organise the revolutionaries were taken by Aurobindo Ghosh, his brother Barin Ghosh, Bhupendranath Datta, Lal Bal Pal and Subodh Chandra Mullick when they formed the Jugantar party in April 1906. Jugantar was created as an inner circle of the Anushilan Samiti, which was already present in Bengal mainly as a fitness club.

Bengal

Anushilan Samiti

Established by Pramathanath Mitra it became one of the most organised revolutionary associations, especially in the Eastern Bengal where the Dhaka Anushilan Samiti had several branches and carried out major activities. Jugantar was initially formed by an inner circle of the Kolkata Anushilan Samiti, like the Palmach of Haganah. In the 1920s, the Kolkata faction supported Gandhi in the Non-Cooperation Movement and many of the leaders held high posts in Congress. The Anushilan Samati had over five hundred branches.Indians living in America and Canada had established the Gadar organization

Jugantar

Barin Ghosh was the main leader. Along with 21 revolutionaries including Bagha Jatin, he started to collect arms and explosives and manufactured bombs. The headquarters of Jugantar was located at 93/a Bowbazar Street, Kolkata.

Some senior members of the group were sent abroad for political and military training. One of them, Hemchandra Kanungo obtained his training in Paris. After returning to Kolkata he set up a combined religious school and bomb factory at a garden house in Maniktala suburb of Calcutta. However, the attempted murder of district Judge Kingsford of Muzaffarpur by Khudiram Bose and Prafulla Chaki (30

April 1908) initiated a police investigation that led to the arrest of many of the revolutionaries.

Bagha Jatin was one of the top leaders in Jugantar. He was arrested, along with several other leaders, in connection with the Howrah-Sibpur Conspiracy case. They were tried for treason, the charge being that they had incited various regiments of the army against the ruler.

Jugantar, along with other revolutionary groups, and aided by Indians abroad, planned an armed revolt against the British rulers during the First World War. This plan largely depended on the clandestine landing of German arms and ammunitions in the Indian coast. This plan came to be known as the *Indo-German Plot.* However, the planned revolt did not materialise.

After the First World War Jugantar supported Gandhi in the Non-Cooperation Movement and many of their leaders were in the Congress. Still, the group continued its revolutionary activities, a notable event being the Chittagong armoury raid.

Badal-Dinesh being its members.

Uttar Pradesh

Hindustan Socialist Republican Association

Hindustan Republican Association (HRA) was established in October 1924 in Kanpur, Uttar Pradesh by revolutionaries like Ramprasad Bismil, Jogesh Chatterjee, Chandrashekhar Azad, Yogendra Shukla and Sachindranath Sanyal. The aim of the party was to organise armed revolution to end the colonial rule and establish a *Federal Republic of the United States of India*. The Kakori train robbery was a notable act of mutiny by this group. The Kakori case led to the hanging of Ashfaqullah Khan, Ramprasad Bismil, Roshan Singh, Rajendra Lahiri. The Kakori case was a major setback for the group. However, the group was soon reorganised under the leadership of Chandrashekhar Azad and with members like Bhagat Singh, Bhagwati Charan Vohra and Sukhdev on 9 and 10 September 1928– and the group was now christened Hindustan Socialist Republican Association (HSRA).

In Lahore on 17 December 1928, Bhagat Singh, Azad and Rajguru assassinated Saunders, a police official involved in deadly lathi-charge on Lala Lajpat Rai. Bhagat Singh and Batukeshwar Dutt threw a bomb inside the Central Legislative Assembly. The Assembly Bomb Case trial followed. Bhagat Singh, Sukhdev Thapar and Shivaram Rajguru were hanged on 23 March 1931.

Maharashtra

Kotwal Dasta

Veer Bhai Kotwal alias Veer Bhai Kotwal during [Quit India Movement] formed group of underground mercenaries called "Kotwal Dasta", a parallel government in the Karjat taluka of Thane district. They were about 50 in numbers including farmers and voluntary school teachers. They decided to cut down the electric pylons supplying electricity to Mumbai city. From September 1942 through November 1942 they felled 11 pylons, paralyzing the industries and railways.

South India

The uprising against the British was evidenced at Halagali (Mudhol taluk of Bagalkot district). The prince of Mudhol, Ghorpade, had accepted British overlordship. But the Bedas (hunters), a martial community, were seething with dissatisfaction under the new dispensation. The British proclaimed the Disarming Act of 1857 whereby men possessing fire arms had to register them and secure a license before 10 November 1857. Babaji Nimbalkar, a soldier thrown out of job from Satara Court, had advised these people not to lose their hereditary right to own arms.

One of the leaders of the Bedas, Jadgia, was invited by the administrator at Mudhol and was persuaded to secure a license on 11 November, though Jadgia had not asked for it. The administrator's expectation that others would follow Jadgia was belied. So he sent his agents to Halagali on 15 and 20 November and again on 21. But the entreaties of the agents did not succeed, and the agents sent on 21 November were attacked by Jadgia and Baalya, another leader, and they were forced to return. Another agent sent on 25 November was not allowed to enter the village.

Meanwhile, the Bedas and other armed men from the neighbouring villages of Mantur, Boodni and Alagundi assembled at Halagali. The administrator reported the matter to Major Malcolm, the Commander at the nearby army headquarters, who sent Col. Seton Karr to Halagali on 29 November.

The insurgents, numbering 500, did not allow the British to enter Halagali. There was a fight during the night. On 30 November, Major Malcolm came with 29th Regiment from Bagalkot. They set fire to the village and many insurgents died, including Babaji Nimbalkar. The British, who had a bigger army and better arms, arrested 290 insurgents; and of those 29 were tried and 11 were hanged at Mudhol on 11 December, and six others, including Jadagia and Baalya were hanged at Halagali on 14 December 1857. No prince or jagirdar was involved in this uprising, but it was the common soldiers. Violent revolutionary activities never took firm root in South India. The only violent act attributed to the revolutionaries was the assassination of Collector of Tirunelveli (Tinnevelly). On 17 June 1911, the Collector of Tirunelveli, Robert Ashe, was killed by R. Vanchi Aiyer, who subsequently committed suicide, which was the only instance of a political assassination by a revolutionary in South India.

Outside India

India House

The India House was an informal Indian nationalist organization that existed in London between 1905 and 1910. Initially begun by Shyamji Krishna Varma as a residence in Highgate, in North London, for Indian students to promote nationalist views and work, the house became a centre for intellectual political activities, and rapidly developed to be an organization that became a meeting ground for radical nationalists among Indian students in Britain at the time, and of the most prominent centers for revolutionary Indian nationalism outside India. *The Indian Sociologist* published by the house was a noted platform for anti-colonial work and was banned in India as "seditious literature".

The India house was the beginnings of a number of noted Indian revolutionaries and nationalists, most famously V.D. Savarkar, as well as others of the like of V.N. Chatterjee, Lala Har Dayal, V.V.S. Iyer, The house came to be the focus of Scotland Yard's work against Indian seditionists, as well as the focus of work for the nascent Indian Political Intelligence Office. India house ceased to be potent organisation after its liquidation in the wake of the assassination of William Hutt Curzon Wyllie by a member of the India House by the name of Madan Lal Dhingra. This event marked the beginnings of London Police's crackdown on the activities of the house and a number of its activists and patrons, including Shyamji Krishna Varma and Bhikaji Cama moved to Europe from where they carried on works in support of Indian nationalism. Some Indian students, including Har Dayal, moved to the United States. The network that the House founded was key in the nationalist revolutionary conspiracy in India during World War I.

Gadar Party

Gadar party was a predominantly Sikh organization that started operating abroad in 1913 "with the view to do-away with the British rule in India". The party collaborated with revolutionaries inside India and helped them get arms and ammunition. Lala Hardayal was a prominent leader of the party and promoter of the Gadar newspaper. The *Komagata Maru* incident in 1914 inspired several thousand Indians residing in the USA to sell their businesses and rush home to participate in the anti-British activities in India. The party had active members in India, Mexico, Japan, China, Singapore, Thailand, Philippines, Malaya, Indo-China and Eastern and Southern Africa. During World War I, it was among the chief participants of the Hindu German Conspiracy.

Berlin Committee

The "Berlin committee for Indian independence" was established in 1915 by Virendra Nath Chattopadhya, including Bhupendra Nath Dutt & Lala Hardayal under "Zimmerman plan" with the full backing of German foreign office.

Their goal was mainly to achieve the following four objectives: 1: Mobilize Indian revolutionaries abroad. 2: Incite rebellion among

Indian troops stationed. abroad. 3: Send volunteers and arms to India. 4: Even to Organized an armed invasion of British India to gain India's independence. and sent British back to home

Pre World War I

Alipore bomb conspiracy case

Several leaders of the Jugantar party including Aurobindo Ghosh were arrested in connection with bomb-making activities in Kolkata. Several of the activists were deported to the Andaman Cellular Jail.

Howrah gang case

Most of the eminent Jugantar leaders including Bagha Jatin alias Jatindra Nath Mukherjee who were not arrested earlier, were arrested in 1910, in connection with the murder of Shamsul Alam. Thanks to Bagha Jatin's new policy of a decentralised federated action, most of the accused were released in 1911.

Delhi-Lahore conspiracy case

The Delhi Conspiracy case, also known as the Delhi-Lahore Conspiracy, hatched in 1912, planned to assassinate the then Viceroy of India, Lord Hardinge, on the occasion of transferring the capital of British India from Calcutta to New Delhi.

Involving revolutionary underground in Bengal and headed by Rashbehari Bose along with Sachin Sanyal, the conspiracy culminated on the attempted assassination on 23 December 1912 when a home-made bomb was thrown into the Viceroys's Howdah when the ceremonial procession moved through the Chandni Chowk suburb of Delhi. The Viceroy escaped with his injuries, along with Lady Hardinge, although the Mahout was killed.

In the aftermath of the event, efforts were made to destroy the Bengali and Punabi revolutionary underground, which came under intense pressure for sometime. Rash Behari successfully evaded capture for nearly three years, becoming actively involved in the Ghadar conspiracy before it was uncovered, and fleeing to Japan in 1916.

The investigations in the aftermath of the assassination attempt led to the Delhi Conspiracy trial. Although Basant Kumar Biswas was convicted of having thrown the bcmb and executed, along with Amir Chand and Avadh Behari for their roles in the conspiracy, the true identity of the person who threw the bomb is not known to this day.

SATYAGRAHA, MONTAGU-CHELMSFORD REFORMS, JALLIANWALLA BAGH: 1917–1919

Gandhi made his political debut in India in 1917 in Champaran district in Bihar, near the Nepal border, where he was invited by a group of disgruntled tenant farmers who, for many years, had been forced into planting indigo (for dyes) on a portion of their land and then selling it at below-market prices to the British planters who had leased them the land. Upon his arrival in the district, Gandhi was joined by other agitators, including a young Congress leader,Rajendra Prasad, from Bihar, who would become a loyal supporter of Gandhi and go on to play a prominent role in the Indian freedom movement. When Gandhi was ordered to leave by the local British authorities, he refused on moral grounds, setting up his refusal as a form of individual Satyagraha. Soon, under pressure from the Viceroy in Delhi who was anxious to maintain domestic peace during war-time, the provincial government rescinded Gandhi's expulsion order, and later agreed to an official enquiry into the case. Although, the British planters eventually gave in, they were not won over to the farmers' cause, and thereby did not produce the optimal outcome of a Satyagraha that Gandhi had hoped for; similarly, the farmers themselves, although pleased at the resolution, responded less than enthusiastically to the concurrent projects of rural empowerment and education that Gandhi had inaugurated in keeping with his ideal of *swaraj*. The following year Gandhi launched two more Satyagrahas – both in his native Gujarat – one in the rural Kaira district where land-owning farmers were protesting increased land-revenue and the other in the city of Ahmedabad, where workers in an Indian-owned textile mill were distressed about their low wages. The satyagraha in Ahmedabad took the form of Gandhi fasting and supporting the workers in a strike, which eventually led to a settlement. In Kaira, in contrast, although the farmers' cause received publicity from Gandhi's presence, the satyagraha itself, which consisted of the farmers' collective decision to withhold payment, was not immediately successful, as the British authorities refused to back down. The agitation in Kaira gained for Gandhi another lifelong lieutenant in Sardar Vallabhbhai Patel, who had organised the farmers, and who too would go on to play a leadership role in the Indian freedom movement. Champaran, Kaira, and Ahmedabad were important milestones in the history of Gandhi's new methods of social protest in India.

In 1916, in the face of new strength demonstrated by the nationalists with the signing of the Lucknow Pact and the founding of the Home Rule leagues, and the realisation, after the disaster in the Mesopotamian campaign, that the war would likely last longer, the new Viceroy, Lord Chelmsford, cautioned that the Government of India needed to be more responsive to Indian opinion. Towards the end of the year, after discussions with the government in London, he suggested that the British demonstrate their good faith – in light of the Indian war role – through a number of public actions, including awards of titles and honours to princes, granting of commissions in the army to Indians, and removal of the much-reviled cotton excise duty, but, most importantly, an announcement of Britain's future plans for India and an indication of some concrete steps.

After more discussion, in August 1917, the new LiberalSecretary of State for India, Edwin Montagu, announced the British aim of "increasing association of Indians in every branch of the administration, and the gradual development of self-governing institutions, with a view to the progressive realisation of responsible government in India as an integral part of the British Empire." Although the plan envisioned limited self-government at first only in the provinces – with India emphatically within the British Empire – it represented the first British proposal for any form of representative government in a non-white colony.

Earlier, at the onset of World War I, the reassignment of most of the British army in India to Europe and Mesopotamia, had led the previous Viceroy, Lord Harding, to worry about the "risks involved in denuding India of troops."

Revolutionary violence had already been a concern in British India; consequently, in 1915, to strengthen its powers during what it saw was a time of increased vulnerability, the Government of India passed the Defence of India Act, which allowed it to intern politically dangerous dissidents without due process, and added to the power it already had – under the 1910 Press Act – both to imprison journalists without trial and to censor the press. It was under the Defence of India act that the Ali brothers were imprisoned in 1916, and Annie Besant, a European woman, and ordinarily more problematic to imprison, in 1917.

Now, as constitutional reform began to be discussed in earnest, the British began to consider how new moderate Indians could be brought into the fold of constitutional politics and, simultaneously, how the hand of established constitutionalists could be strengthened. However, since the Government of India wanted to ensure against any sabotage of the reform process by extremists, and since its reform plan was devised during a time when extremist violence had ebbed as a result of increased governmental control, it also began to consider how some of its war-time powers could be extended into peace time.

Consequently, in 1917, even as Edwin Montagu, announced the new constitutional reforms, a committee chaired by a British judge, Mr. S. A. T. Rowlatt, was tasked with investigating "revolutionary conspiracies," with the unstated goal of extending the government's war-time powers. The Rowlatt committee presented its report in July 1918 and identified three regions of conspiratorial insurgency: Bengal, the Bombay presidency, and the Punjab. To combat subversive acts in these regions, the committee recommended that the government use emergency powers akin to its war-time authority, which included the ability to try cases of sedition by a panel of three judges and without juries, exaction of securities from suspects, governmental overseeing of residences of suspects, and the power for provincial governments to arrest and detain suspects in short-term detention facilities and without trial.

With the end of World War I, there was also a change in the economic climate. By year's end 1919, 1.5 million Indians had served in the armed services in either combatant or non-combatant roles, and India had provided £146 million in revenue for the war. The increased taxes coupled with disruptions in both domestic and international trade had the effect of approximately doubling the index of overall prices in India between 1914 and 1920. Returning war veterans, especially in the Punjab, created a growing unemployment crisis, and post-war inflation led to food riots in Bombay, Madras, and Bengal provinces, a situation that was made only worse by the failure of the 1918–19 monsoon and by profiteering and speculation. The global influenza epidemic and the Bolshevik Revolution of 1917 added to the general jitters; the former among the population already experiencing economic woes, and the latter among government officials, fearing a similar revolution in India.

To combat what it saw as a coming crisis, the government now drafted the Rowlatt committee's recommendations into two Rowlatt Bills. Although the bills were authorised for legislative consideration by Edwin Montagu, they were done so unwillingly, with the accompanying declaration, "I loathe the suggestion at first sight of preserving the Defence of India Act in peace time to such an extent as Rowlatt and his friends think necessary."

In the ensuing discussion and vote in the Imperial Legislative Council, all Indian members voiced opposition to the bills. The Government of India was, nevertheless, able to use of its "official majority" to ensure passage of the bills early in 1919. However, what it passed, in deference to the Indian opposition, was a lesser version of the first bill, which now allowed extrajudicial powers, but for a period of exactly three years and for the prosecution solely of "anarchical and revolutionary movements," dropping entirely the second bill involving modification the Indian Penal Code. Even so, when it was passed, the new Rowlatt Act aroused widespread indignation throughout India, and brought Gandhi to the forefront of the nationalist movement.

Meanwhile, Montagu and Chelmsford themselves finally presented their report in July 1918 after a long fact-finding trip through India the previous winter. After more discussion by the government and parliament in Britain, and another tour by the Franchise and Functions Committee for the purpose of identifying who among the Indian population could vote in future elections, the Government of India Act 1919 (also known as the Montagu-Chelmsford Reforms) was passed in December 1919. The new Act enlarged both the provincial and Imperial legislative councils and repealed the Government of India's recourse to the "official majority" in unfavourable votes. Although departments like defence, foreign affairs, criminal law, communications, and income-tax were retained by the Viceroy and the central government in New Delhi, other departments like public health, education, land-revenue, local self-government were transferred to the provinces.

The provinces themselves were now to be administered under a new dyarchical system, whereby some areas like education, agriculture, infrastructure development, and local self-government became the preserve of Indian ministers and legislatures, and ultimately the Indian electorates, while others like irrigation, land-revenue, police, prisons, and control of media remained within the purview of the British governor and his executive council. The new Act also made it easier for Indians to be admitted into the civil service and the army officer corps. A greater number of Indians were now enfranchised, although, for voting at the national level, they constituted only 10% of the total adult male population, many of whom were still illiterate.

In the provincial legislatures, the British continued to exercise some control by setting aside seats for special interests they considered cooperative or useful. In particular, rural candidates, generally sympathetic to British rule and less confrontational, were assigned more seats than their urban counterparts. Seats were also reserved for non-Brahmins, landowners, businessmen, and college graduates. The principal of "communal representation," an integral part of the Minto-Morley reforms, and more recently of the Congress-Muslim League Lucknow Pact, was reaffirmed, with seats being reserved for Muslims, Sikhs, Indian Christians, Anglo-Indians, and domiciled Europeans, in both provincial and Imperial legislative councils. The

Montagu-Chelmsford reforms offered Indians the most significant opportunity yet for exercising legislative power, especially at the provincial level; however, that opportunity was also restricted by the still limited number of eligible voters, by the small budgets available to provincial legislatures, and by the presence of rural and special interest seats that were seen as instruments of British control.

Its scope was unsatisfactory to the Indian political leadership, famously expressed by Annie Beasant as something "unworthy of England to offer and India to accept".

The Jallianwala Bagh massacre or "Amritsar massacre", took place in the Jallianwala Bagh public garden in the predominantly Sikh northern city ofAmritsar. After days of unrest Brigadier-General Reginald E.H. Dyer forbade public meetings and on Sunday 13 April 1919 fifty British Indian Army soldiers commanded by Dyer began shooting at an unarmed gathering of thousands of men, women, and children without warning. Casualty estimates vary widely, with the Government of India reporting 379 dead, with 1,100 wounded. The Indian National Congress estimated three times the number of dead. Dyer was removed from duty but he became a celebrated hero in Britain among people with connections to the Raj. Historians consider the episode was a decisive step towards the end of British rule in India.

Noncooperation, *Khilafat*, Simon Commission, Jinnah's fourteen points: 1920s

In 1920, after the British government refused to back down, Gandhi began his campaign of noncooperation, prompting many Indians to return British awards and honours, to resign from civil service, and to again boycott British goods. In addition, Gandhi reorganised the Congress, transforming it into a mass movement and opening its membership to even the poorest Indians. Although Gandhi halted the noncooperation movement in 1922 after the violentincident at Chauri Chaura, the movement revived again, in the mid-1920s.

The visit, in 1928, of the British Simon Commission, charged with instituting constitutional reform in India, resulted in widespread protests throughout the country. Earlier, in 1925, non-violent protests of the Congress had resumed too, this time in Gujarat, and led by Patel, who organised farmers to refuse payment of increased land taxes; the success of this protest, the Bardoli Satyagraha, brought Gandhi back into the fold of active politics.

Round Table Conferences, Government of India Act: 1929–1937

At its annual session in Lahore, the Indian National Congress, under the presidency of Jawaharlal Nehru, issued a demand for *Purna Swaraj* (Hindi: "complete independence"), or Purna Swarajya. The declaration was drafted by the Congress Working Committee, which included Gandhi, Nehru, Patel, and Chakravarthi Rajagopalachari. Gandhi subsequently led an expanded movement of civil disobedience, culminating in 1930 with the Salt Satyagraha, in which thousands of Indians defied the tax on salt, by marching to the sea and making their own salt by evaporating seawater. Although, many, including Gandhi, were arrested, the British government eventually gave in, and in 1931 Gandhi travelled to London to negotiate new reform at the Round Table Conferences.

In local terms British control rested on the Indian Civil Service, but it faced growing difficulties. Fewer and fewer young men in Britain were interested in joining, and the continuing distrust of Indians resulted in a declining base in terms of quality and quantity. By 1945 Indians were numerically dominant in the ICS and at issue was loyal divided between the Empire and independence. The finances of the Raj depended on land taxes, and these became problematic in the 1930s. Epstein argues that after 1919 it became harder and harder to collect the land revenue. The Raj's suppression of civil disobedience after 1934 temporarily increased the power of the revenue agents but after 1937 they were forced by the new Congress-controlled provincial governments to hand back confiscated land. Again the outbreak of war strengthened them, in the face of the Quit India movement the revenue collectors had to rely on military force and by 1946–47 direct British control was rapidly disappearing in much of the countryside.

In 1935, after the Round Table Conferences, Parliament passed the Government of India Act 1935, which authorised the establishment of independent legislative assemblies in all provinces of British India, the creation of a central government incorporating both the British provinces and the princely states, and the protection of Muslim minorities. The future Constitution of independent India was based on this act. However, it divided the electorate into 19 religious and social categories, e.g., Moslems, Sikhs, Indian Christians, Depressed Classes, Landholders, Commerce and Industry, Europeans, Anglo-Indians, etc., each of which was given separate representation in the Provincial Legislative Assemblies. A voter could cast a vote only for candidates in his own category.

The 1935 Act provided for more autonomy for Indian provinces, with the goal of cooling off nationalist sentiment. The act provided for a national parliament and an executive branch under the purview of the British government, but the rulers of the prıncely states managed to block its implementation. These states remained under the full control of their hereditary rulers, with no popular government. To prepare for elections Congress built up its grass roots membership from 473,000 in 1935 to 4.5 million in 1939.

In the 1937 elections Congress won victories in seven of the eleven provinces of British India. Congress governments, with wide powers, were formed in these provinces. The widespread voter support for the Indian National Congress surprised Raj officials, who previously had seen the Congress as a small elitist body.

WORLD WAR I : INDO-GERMAN JOINT MOVEMENT

The Indo-German movement, also referred to as the Hindu-German Conspiracy or the Ghadar movement (or Ghadr conspiracy), was formulated during World War I between Indian Nationalists in India, United States and Germany, the Irish Republicans, and the German Foreign office to initiate a Pan-Indian rebellion against The Raj with German support between 1914 and 1917, during World War I. The most famous amongst a number of plots planned to foment unrest and trigger a Pan-Indian mutiny in February 1915, in the

British Indian Army from Punjab to Singapore, to overthrow The Raj in the Indian subcontinent. This conspiracy was ultimately thwarted at the last moment as British intelligence successfully infiltrated the Ghadarite movement and arrested key figures. The failed Singapore mutiny remains a famous part of this plot while mutinies in other smaller units and garrisons within India were also crushed.

World War I began with an unprecedented outpouring of loyalty and goodwill towards the United Kingdom from within the mainstream political leadership, contrary to initial British fears of an Indian revolt. India contributed massively to the British war effort by providing men and resources. About 1.3 million Indian soldiers and labourers served in Europe, Africa, and the Middle East, while both the Indian government and the princes sent large supplies of food, money, and ammunition. However, Bengal and Punjab remained hotbeds of anti colonial activities. Terrorism in Bengal, increasingly closely linked with the unrests in Punjab, was significant enough to nearly paralyse the regional administration. With outlines of German links with the Indian revolutionary movement already in place as early as 1912, the main conspiracy was formulated between the Ghadar Party in United States, the Berlin Committee in Germany, Indian revolutionary underground in India, Sinn Féin and the German Foreign Office through the consulate in San Francisco at the beginning of World War I. A number of failed attempts were made at mutiny, among them the February mutiny plan and the Singapore mutiny. This movement was suppressed by means of a massive international counter-intelligence operation and draconian political acts (including the Defence of India act 1915) that lasted nearly ten years. Other notable events that formed a part of the conspiracy include the Annie Larsen arms plot, the Mission to Kabul that also attempted to rally Afghanistan against British India. The Mutiny of the Connaught Rangers in India, as well as by some accounts, the Black Tom explosion in 1916 are also considered minor events linked to the conspiracy.

The Indo-Irish-German alliance and the conspiracy were the target of a worldwide intelligence effort by the British intelligence agencies which was ultimately successful in preventing further attempts and plans, and in the aftermath of the Annie Larsen affair, successfully directed the American intelligence agencies to arrest key figures at the time she entered World War I in 1917. The conspiracy led to the Lahore conspiracy case in India and the Hindu German Conspiracy Trial in the USA, of which the latter at the time was one of the longest and most expensive trials in that country. Largely subdued and suppressed by the end of the war, the movement posed a significant threat to British India during World War I and its aftermath, and was a major factor guiding The Raj's India policy.

Tehrek e Reshmi Rumal

During the war, the Pan-Islamist movement also attempted to overthrow the Raj, and came to form a close liaison with the Indo-German Conspiracy. Out of the Deobandi movement arose the Tehrek-e-Reshmi Rumal. The Deobandi leaders attempted to begin a pan-Islamic insurrection in British India during World War I by seeking support from Ottoman Turkey, Imperial Germany, Afghanistan.

The plot was uncovered by Punjab CID with the capture of letters from Ubaidullah Sindhi, one of the Deobandi leaders then in Afghanistan, to Mahmud al Hasan another leaders then in Persia. The letters were written in Silk cloth, hence the name of the Silk Letter Conspiracy.

Between the wars

Chittagong armoury raid

Surya Sen led Indian revolutionaries to raid the armoury of police and auxiliary forces and to cut all communication lines in Chittagong on 18 April 1930. After successfully completing the raid, revolutionaries establish Provincial National Government of India, after this in deadly clash with Government troops in Jalalabad Hill, revolutionaries scattered themselves in small groups. and Some revolutionaries were soon killed or arrested in a gun-fight with the police. Scores of Government officials, policeman were also killed. Pritilata Waddedar led the attack on European club in Chittagong in 1932. Surya Sen was arrested in 1933 and was hanged on 8 January 1934.

Central Assembly Bomb Case (1929)

Bhagat Singh and Batukeshwar Dutt threw a bomb in the assembly house along with leaflets stating their revolutionary philosophy – 'to make the deaf hear'. Bhagat Singh, Sukhdev and Rajguru were hanged and several other faced the verdict of imprisonment. Batukeshwar Dutt outlived all his comrades and died in July 1965 in Delhi. All of them cremated in Ferozpur (Punjab, India).

Baikuntha Shukla, the great nationalist was hanged for murdering Phanindrananth Ghosh who had become a government approver which led to hanging of Bhagat Singh, Sukhdev and Rajguru. He was a nephew of Yogendra Shukla. Baikunth Shukla was also initiated into the independence struggle at a young age taking active part in the 'Salt Satyagraha' of 1930. He was associated with revolutionary organisations like the Hindustan Seva Dal and Hindustan Socialist Republican Association. The execution of the great Indian revolutionaries Bhagat Singh, Rajguru and Sukhdev in 1931 as a result of their trial in the 'Lahore conspiracy case' was an event that shook the entire country. Phanindra Nath Ghosh, hitherto a key member of the Revolutionary Party had treacherously betrayed the cause by turning an approver, giving evidence, which led to the execution. Baikunth was commissioned to plan the execution of Ghosh as an act of ideological vendetta which he carried out successfully on 9 November 1932. He was arrested and tried for the killing. Baikunth was convicted and hanged in Gaya Central Jail on 14 May 1934. He was only 28 years old.

On 27 February 1931, Chandrasekar Azad died in a shootout when cornered by the police.

It is unclear of the eventual fate of the Association, but the common understanding is that it disbanded with the death of Chandrashekar Azad and the hanging of its popular activists: Bhagat Singh, Sukhdev and Rajguru.

Dalhousie Square Bomb Case

A bomb was thrown on the Calcutta Police Commissioner, Charles Tegart on 25 August 1930.

Kakori train robbery

Chandrasekhar Azad, Ramprasad Bismil, Jogesh Chatterjee, Ashfaqullah Khan, Banwari Lal and their accomplices participated in the robbery of treasury money that was being transported by train. The looting took place between Kakori station and Alamnagar, within 40 miles (64 km) of Lucknow on 9 August 1925. Police started an intense man-hunt and arrested a large number of rebels and tried them in the Kakori case. Ashfaqullah Khan, Ramprasad Bismil, Roshan Singh, Rajendra Lahiri were hanged, four others were sent to the Cellular Jail in Port Blair, Andaman for life and seventeen others were sentenced to long terms of imprisonment.

World War II

The scenario changed with the years. The British were thinking to quit India and religious politics came into play. The basic political background of revolutionary ideas seemed to evolve in a new direction. The organised revolutionary movements can be said to have nearly ceased by 1936, apart from some stray sparks, like the killing of Sir Michael O'Dwyer, generally held responsible for the Amritsar Massacre, on 13 March 1940, by Udham Singh in London.

During the Quit India movement of 1942, several other activities took place in different parts of India. However, those were discrete occurrences and hardly any large scale planned terrorism took place that could shake the British administration.

Meanwhile, Subhas Chandra Bose was organising an Indian National Army outside India and leading the army towards India, while at the same time the Congress was negotiating with the British. Finally India was independent on 15 August 1947, virtually by non-violence against the British but with much of bloodshed, rioting and violence among the countrymen (and near-future neighbours) during the partition, which was quite shocking to the past revolutionaries and also to Gandhi.

Many revolutionaries participated in mainstream politics and joined political parties like the Congress and, especially, the communist parties and took part in the parliamentary democracy that was India.

On the other hand, many past revolutionaries, being released from captivity, led the lives of common men.

FARMERS' MOVEMENTS

The farmers in India had to do a great struggle in all the states to get rid of exploitation by the Jagirdars and zamindars. Some of the movements were successful but some failed. The farmer movements in 1907 under the leadership of Sardar Ajit Singh and in 1921 under Sardar Vallabhbhai Patel were a grand success but the farmers were subjected to great sufferings in Chauri Chaura, Avadh and Mopla farmer movements.

At the global level the French Revolution had changed the course of history. Since then it was the working class which became the vanguard of revolution in Europe. But when during the first half of the 20th century, national liberation struggles started against colonisation, there was very little industry in the colonies and their working class, if it existed at all, was still in infancy. So the impetus for these struggles had to come from somewhere else. It was Mao's peasant revolution in China which became a role model for national liberation movements in many a colony, including India.

Farmer Movements in Punjab

In India it was in Punjab that India's first farmers' movement emerged. The role played by Ghadar party, led by Raja Mahendra Pratap, in the political awakening of India was an important step. The Sikhs of Punjab were the first to migrate to the United States and Canada in the 19th century. They financed and helped the formation of Ghadar party which when gave the call to Indians abroad to return home and fight British imperialism, had its call immediately heeded to. The majority of those who did return--8000 of them--comprised Punjab's (Sikhs). Despite its apparent failure, the Ghadar Movement was to have a powerful impact on Punjab politics and especially on the peasants. It established a tradition of militant and secular anti-imperialism, enriched in subsequent years by social radicalism, which was to continue to inspire subsequent generations. The peasant conferences were held in Lahore, Lyallpur and other places of West Punjab--the most famous of them being 1938-39 Long Morcha in Lahore when peasants from all over Punjab courted arrests for nine months in front of the assembly building.

The slogan of Pagri Sambhal O' Jatta (Hold your head high, O peasant) was first raised at a mass gathering in Lyallpur in 1907. Ten Thousand people--the Hindus, the Muslims and the Sikhs alike--attended this gathering.

Farmers' Movements in Gujarat

Mahatma Gandhi had led two great revolts of communities of poor Indian farmers against the tyranny of the British government and allied landlords in Champaran, Bihar, and Kheda, Gujarat. Success in both struggles had helped win the farmers economic and civil rights, and electrified India's people.

In 1920, the Indian National Congress under Gandhi's leadership launched the Non-Cooperation Movement. Millions of Indians revolted against the British, boycotting the courts, government services, schools and disavowing titles, pensions and British clothes and goods. The freedom fighters, known as Satyagrahis, peacefully protested authoritarian British laws, and called for India's independence. Many thousands were beaten, tortured and arrested.

Farmer Movements in Rajasthan

Rajasthan is known as the land of kings and palaces and whose history is replete with encomium of their kings, the land known for "Sati", the land known for its vast tracts of deserts was witness to a history in making, the successful agitation of farmers and peasants for their right to livelihood.

The twenty-two princely states of erstwhile Rajputana state did not form a common political collectivity which can be termed as a unified political action model. Each state had its own territorial area, which was exclusive politically in that it had its separate administration nag and army. Each state retained its cultural and linguistic distinctiveness. Political authority varied from ruler to ruler depending upon the terms of contract or covenant with the paramount power dating back to the period of subsidiary alliance of Lord Wellesley.

Obviously in a state like this, freedom movement was bound to be divided and segmented, depending upon the degree of unity and cohesiveness among political players in each state. The two states of Jaipur and Jodhpur provided differential patterns of political movements.

Justice Kan Singh Parihar, the retired Judge of High Court of Rajasthan, has written about exploitation of farmers by Jagirdars prior to Independence as under:

"Every thing that the Kisan had, never treated as his own. In Jagir areas all cultivators were really landless. There was no tenancy law and one could be thrown away from the land one cultivated at the pleasure of Jagirdar, his "malik". In most of the Jagirs a Jagirdar would in the first instance be taking fifty percent of the produce.

This would be taken by actual division of the produce on the thrashing floor or by appraisal of the standing crop (kunta). Then over and above the share of the produce the Kisan had to pay numerous "lags" or cesses.

Together with the share of the produce known as "Hasil" these cesses meant that the Kisans had to part with more than eighty percent of their produce. The findings of the Sukhdeonarain Committee in the years 1940-42 bear this out. If a Kisan had to marry his daughter he had to pay "Chavri Lag" if he held a dinner then a "Kansa Lag"; if members of the family separated then "Dhunwa Lag" and so on. If the Jagirdar had a guest then fodder for his mount had to be supplied. Then there was "begar" that is forced labour, for tilling the personal lands of the Jagirdar. The homestead in which the Kisan lived in the Abadi had to be vacated in case he ceased cultivating the land. He could not alienate the plot to anyone."

THE NATIONALIST MOVEMENT UNDER GANDHIJI

Mohandas Karamchand Gandhi took control of the national movement in 1919. With this, the third and significant phase of Indian nationalism began and which continued till independence. Gandhian philosophy emphasized the strategy of Satyagraha and Ahimsa in fighting against the British. In his struggle against the racist authorities of South Africa, Gandhi evolved the technique of Satyagraha based on truth and non-violence.

Gandhi showed the people a new way of fighting injustice without violence, for what one believed to be right and he called this "Satyagraha." The Swadeshi program of Gandhi was based on the belief that political freedom was closely liked, with social and economic changes and it meant the use of things belonging to one's own country partic-ularly stressing the replacement of foreign machine-made goods with Indian handmade cloth. Gandhian philosophy consisted non-violent resistance and, when applied to the Indian scene, it served to bring millions of people into the National movement.

The Rowlatt Act was met with a wide protest from the different sections of Indian society. As a reaction, the British government resorted to lathi charges and firings in many places. It eventually resulted in the Jallianwala Bagh Massacre that was the reflec-tion of General Dyer's unexampled brutality and deliberately calculated massacre. The Khilafat Movement was a protest against the injustices done to Turkey after the World War I. In fact, it became a part of the Indian National Movement.

The Congress leaders joined the Khilafat agitation and helped in organizing the same throughout the country and it was the first countrywide popular movement. Under the leadership of Gandhi, the Congress in a special session at Calcutta in 1920 adopted the new program of non-violent non-cooperation movement. The aims of the non-cooperation movement were to redress the wrongs done to Punjab and Turkey, and the attainment of Swaraj. It involved the surrender of the titles and honorary offices and resignations from nominated posts in the local bodies. The participants of the non-cooperation movement were not to attend Government Levies. Durbars and other official and semi-official functions held by the Government officials or in their honor.

They were to withdraw their children gradually from the schools and colleges and establish national schools and colleges. They were to boycott gradually the British courts and establish private arbitra-tion courts. Ahimsa or non-violence was to be strictly observed by the participants of the non-cooperation movement and they were not to give up Satya or truth under any circumstances. The Non-Cooperation Movement spread among the masses and to the countryside. The peasantry of UP., Bengal, Bihar, Orissa, and Malabar (Northern Kerala) responded to the non-cooperation movement. The tragedy of Chauri Chaura and Gandhi s imprisonment put an end to the non-cooperation movement itself for some time.

An unfortunate development after the calling-off of the non-cooperation movement was the growth of communal tension and the occurrence of communal riots. The growth of communal tendencies hindered the nationalist movement. These sidetracked the atten-tion of people from the need for complete independence from foreign rule. The civil disobedience movement began with the famous Dandi March on 12 March 1930. In this place, Gandhi and his followers made salt in violation of the salt laws. This act was a symbol of the Indians refusal to live under the British-made laws and also under the British rule.

The Civil Disobedience Movement was reflected in the activities of hartals, demonstrations, and the campaign to boycott foreign goods and the refusal to pay taxes. The Indians showed their resistance to the British rule in the form of passive resistance. A remarkable characteristic of the movement was the extensive involvement of women. They took an active part in picketing shops, selling foreign cloth or liquor. They marched shoulder to shoulder with the men in the processions. Gandhi was arrested and the movement continued for two years and the repression of the government was more severe than it had been before.

In May 1934, the entire Civil Disobedience Movement was called off. The resistance involved millions of people in the country, young and old, men and women, and people belonging to all regions and communities. Even though the Congress condemned the Government of India Act, 1935, it decided to participate in the elections to the provincial legislatures that were to take place in 1937. The elections were held in 1937.

The parties that participated in the elections were the Congress, the Muslim League, and others. The North-West Frontier Province, United Provinces, Central Provinces, Bihar, Orissa, Madras, and Bombay were the seven prov-inces wherein the Congress formed its ministries.

The Congress ministries soon after coming to power took some important measures such as the release of political prisoners and the lifting of ban on the newspapers. The widespread dissatisfaction against the British in India resulted in launching of the Quit India movement. "Quit India", the pithiest call to action resounded through-out the country. The British government used the police and the army to suppress the Movement.

The Quit India Movement or the August Revolution marked a new era in the history of Indian National Movement. Though the Quit India Movement was a short-lived one, it exhibited the depth that nationalist feeling had reached in the country.

Besides, it also revealed the great capacity for struggle and sacrifice that the people rendered. It also served as an eye-opener to the British Government about India's attitude to British imperialism. It was a revelation to the British that they cannot dominate over India for long. It was a landmark in India's struggle against British imperialism.

Congress & The Freedom Movement

The 1857 revolt was suppressed. The British Empire in India was saved. Queen Victoria was proclaimed Empress of India and the new policy was ushered in. It was even more reactionary and in the long run proved very harmful. The native princes were now to be used as British tools and propped as bulwark against forces of resistance and progress. Government was no longer to encourage social reform. The benign rule was thus to carefully preserve decaying aristocracies, superstition and warring dogmas and cults. These were to provide the pattern for British imperialism with its foundations laid deep in the religious differences, caste and untouchabilitly and the feudal states and the aristocracy.

Economic and Political Discontent

The policy of economic exploitation, however, became even worse though more subtle. Mass unrest was the inevitable result of the ever growing poverty and helplessness of the peasantry. The common people, Hindus and Muslims, struggled against the terrible oppression, wherever they could and with whatever weapons they could muster. There was a new English educated class which was used to run the Government machinery. I was great admirer of everything Western which lent its support to the Government. The belief of the educated classes in the English tradition of liberal thought and institutions received setbacks as a result of various Government measures.

The Freedom of the press, introduced earlier by Metcalfe, was soon done away with. The vernacular Press was gagged in 1878 and the Bengali *Amrita Bazar Patrika* had to change overnight into an English garb. The Arms Act was passed in 1879. This disillusionment advanced further when the *Illbert* Bill to abolish "Judicial discrimination, based on racial distinction" had to be virtually dropped on account of fierce opposition by the European community and the Civil Service. The Europeans did not hesitate to threaten the Viceroy, Lord Ripon, with violence if the Bill was passed. Indians learned the lesson at this time. In 1853 the first Cotton Mill was established in Bombay. The number of mills rose to 156 by 1880. This was an alarming progress and under pressure of Lancashire, all duties on cotton imports into India were removed in 1882.

Social Renaissance

It was not merely the economic exploitation and the sense of political subjection that gave birth to the Congress. For fifty years and more before the birth of the Congress, the leaven of national rejuvenation had been at work. In fact national life was in a state of ferment as early as in the times of *Rammohan Roy,* who could in a way be regarded as the prophet of Indian Nationalism and the father of modern India. He had a wide vision and a broad outlook. While it is true that the socio-religious condition of his day was the subject of his special attention in his reformist activities, he had nevertheless a keen sense of the grave political wrongs by which his country was afflicted at that time and made a strenuous effort to seek an early redress of those wrongs. Rammohan Roy was born in 1776 and passed away at Bristol in 1833. His name is associated with two great reforms in India, namely, the abolition of Sati and the introduction of Western learning in the country.

In the closing period of his life he chose to visit England and his passion for liberty was so great that when he reached the Cape of Good Hope he insisted on his being carried to a French vessel where he saw the flag of liberty flying, so that he might be able to do homage to that flag, and when he saw the flag he shouted, "Glory, Glory, Glory to the Flag." Although he had gone to England primarily as the ambassador of the Mughal Emperor to plead his cause in London, yet he took the opportunity to place some of the pressing Indian grievances before a Committee of the House of Commons. He submitted three papers, on the Revenue system of India, the Judicial system of India, and the Material condition of India. He was honoured by the East India Company with a public dinner. When in 1832 the Charter Act was before Parliament he vowed that if the Bill was not passed he would give up his residence in the British dominion and reside in America.

The Universities were established in 1858 and the High Courts and the Legislative Councils in India between 1861 and 1863. Just before the "mutiny", the "Widow Re-marriage Act" was passed as also the Act relating to conversion into Christianity. In the sixties of the nineteenth century, an intimate contact was established with Western learning -and literature. Western legal institutions and Parliamentary methods were inaugurated, to mark a new era in the field of law and legislation. The impact of Western civilization on the East could not but leave a deep impress upon the beliefs and sentiments of the Indian people who came directly under its influence. The only parts of the country which had received some education on modem lines were the provinces of Bengal, Bombay and Madras. The number of educated men even in these provinces was small. In the work of settlement that followed the mutiny, these educated men found ample scope for their ambition. These races of *Babus* began to think like their English masters, admired and emulated everything that came from the West. Soon, however, there was a reaction against this process of denationalisation which assumed various forms, some of a synthesis of the West and the East and others of a revivalism going to the past.

BUILDING UP TO THE QUIT INDIA MOVEMENT

Subhas Chandra Bose attempted to lead a radical revival of the Congress and tried to steer it in a more radical and socialist direction. In 1939, he defeated Gandhi's nominee Pattabhi Sitaramayya to be re-elected Congress president. But he was ill-prepared to deal with a campaign of noncooperation launched against him by Gandhi, and resigned a few months later to launch an alternative and more radical platform that eventually became the Forward Block in independent India.

The outbreak of the Second World War opened up a new and more determined phase of the struggle against British rule. In 1939 and 1940, strikes and peasant uprisings reached a fever pitch. In 1941, the Indian National Army (INA) was launched by General Mohan Singh in Malaya with the help of the Japanese. He belonged to Sialkot (Punjab) and had been greatly influenced by the killings of Jallianwala Bagh and hangings of the Ghadar Party members during his younger years.

In 1943, Netaji Subhash Chander Bose (who had always been close to the armed revolutionaries of Bengal) took over the Indian National Army and it was renamed as the Azad Hind Fauj. More than two million Indian civilians living in Southeast Asia responded to his call for "total mobilization". In his army of liberation Punjabi, Muslim, Sikh and Pathan professional soldiers fought side by side with Tamil and Malayalee rubber plantation workers. In his Azad Hind Movement Netaji was able to demonstrate by example how to achieve Hindu-Muslim unity and amity and enable women to get their rightful role in public affairs.

By 1942, the Congress too was compelled to act boldly, and issued the Quit India call in August. The Quit India Movement of 1942 swept across the length and breadth of the country like a mighty tidal wave bringing in its fold people from all walks of life, arousing in them tremendous patriotic fervour and an irresistible urge to act. Volunteers from groups like the Hindu Mahasabha who had all this while remained aloof from the mass struggle joined in as well. Individual industrialists were emboldened too and encouraged strike actions against the British.

The Role of Women

One of the important facets of India's freedom movement was the growing participation of women. Women played an especially crucial role in the economic boycott campaigns and often participated in the noncooperation movement with as much or even greater enthusiasm than their husbands or male relatives.

In rallies organized by the Congress, women attended in large numbers often with little children in tow. Particularly notable was the participation of women in the armed struggle of Bengal. In the group led by Surya Sen, they provided shelter, acted as messengers and custodians of arms, and fought, guns in hand. Pritilata Waddedar died while conducting a raid, while Kalpana Dutt (now Joshi) was arrested and tried along with Surya Sen and given a life sentence. In December 1931, two school girls of Comilla, Santi Ghosh and Suniti Chowdhury, shot dead the District Magistrate.

In February 1932, Bina Das fired point blank at the Governor while receiving her degree at the Convocation. When the entire Congress leadership was put in jail in 1942, women leaders like Aruna Asaf Ali and Sucheta Kripalani emerged with Achyut Patwardhan and Ram Manohar Lohia and others to lead the underground resistance. Usha Mehta ran the Congress radio. Congress socialists, Forward Bloc members, and other armed resistance factions were active in this period, working through underground cells in Mumbai, Pune, Satara, Baroda, and other parts of Gujarat, Karnataka, Kerala, Andhra Pradesh, UP, Bihar and Delhi.

The Revolutionary Peasantry, Adivasis and Dalits

The final phase of the Indian freedom struggle also saw peasant struggles rising to new heights of militancy. Throughout the country, Kisan Sabhas had been active in the 1930s. After the Quit-India call, peasants of all classes joined in the freedom struggle in Eastern UP, Bihar, Midnapur in Bengal, Satara in Maharashtra, and also in Andhra, Gujarat and Kerala. Even some of the Zamindars (landlords) joined in. The Raja of Darbhanga was one of the most supportive of the resisting peasants. Adivasis and landless peasants were particularly heroic in their struggles. Crushed by the inhumane demands of the Zamindari system, they had to fight a dual war-one against the British and the other against the Indian landlords who collaborated with British rule. Amongst the most significant of these struggles were those of Tebhaga, Punnapra Vayalar, the Worli adivasis and above all the historic Telangana peasants armed struggle which was directed against the Nizam of Hyderabad who had collaborated with the British.

During the course of the freedom struggle, the issue of equality for Adivasis and Dalits came up again and again. Phule, Periyar and Ambedkar emerged as amongst the most prominent of the Dalit leaders. The Ghadar movement, the HSRA and later the INA led the way in breaking down caste and communal barriers. The Congress, while open to some reforms, often did not go far enough-leading to well-deserved criticism from the more radical of the Dalit and Adivasi leaders. Nevertheless, virtually all the advanced sections of the freedom struggle came to the conclusion that for India to succeed as a modern nation, the issue of equality for Dalits and Adivasis could not be dismissed.

7

Martyr Bhagat Singh: A Greatest Revolutionary

A freedom fighter, he was considered to be one of the most famous revolutionaries of the *Bharatiya* Independence movement. For this reason, he is often referred to as 'Shaheed' (martyr) *Bhagat* Singh. At such a young age, if anyone was smiling just before being hanged to death, it was Martyr Bhagat Singh. His uncle, Sardar Ajit Singh, as well as his father, were great freedom fighters, so Bhagat Singh grew up in a patriotic atmosphere. At an early age, Bhagat Singh started dreaming of uprooting the British empire. Never afraid of fighting during his childhood, he thought of 'growing guns in the fields', so that he could fight the British. The Ghadar Movement left a deep imprint on his mind. Kartar Singh Sarabha, hanged at the age of 19, became his hero. The massacre at Jallianwala Bagh on 13th April, 1919 drove him to Amritsar, where he kissed the earth sanctified by the martyrs' blood and brought back home a little of the soaked soil. At the age of 16, he used to wonder why so many Bharatiyas could not drive away a fistful of invaders.

In search of revolutionary groups and ideas, he met Sukhdev and Rajguru. Bhagat Singh, along with the help of Chandrashekhar Azad, formed the Hindustan Socialist Republican Army (HSRA). The aim of this *Bharatiya* revolutionary movement was now defined as not only to make Bharat independent, but also to create a socialist Bharat.

A brutal attack by the police on veteran freedom fighter Lala Lajpat Rai at an anti-British procession caused his death on 17th November 1928, in Lahore. Bhagat Singh determined to avenge Lajpat Rai's death by shooting the British official responsible for the killing, Deputy Inspector General Scott. He shot down Assistant Superintendent Saunders instead, mistaking him for Scott.

Then he made a dramatic escape from Lahore to Calcutta and from there to Agra, where he established a bomb factory. The British Government responded to the act by imposing severe measures like the Trades Disputes Bill. It was to protest against the passing of the Bill that he threw bombs in the Central Assembly Hall (now our Loksabha) while the Assembly was in session. The bombs did not hurt anyone, but the noise they made was loud enough to wake up an enslaved Nation from a long sleep. After throwing the bombs, Bhagat Singh and his friend deliberately courted arrest by refusing to run away from the scene. During his trial, Bhagat Singh refused to employ any Defense counsel.

Despite great popular pressure and numerous appeals by political leaders of Bharat, Bhagat Singh, Sukhdev and Rajguru were awarded the death sentence and hanged in the early hours of 23rd March 1931. Their bodies were cremated on the bank of the Sutlej in Ferozepur. Bhagat Singh was just 23 years old at that time. Old timers say that in many places, not a single hearth fire burned that day.

The last paragraph of the leaflet that he distributed (and wrote) in the Assembly Hall said: "We are sorry that we who attach such great sanctity to human life, we who dream of a very glorious future when man will be enjoying perfect peace and full liberty, have been forced to shed human blood. But sacrifice of individuals at the altar of the Revolution will bring freedom to all, rendering exploitation of man by man impossible. *Inquilab Zindabad* (Long live the Revolution)." There was a time when the very mention of the name of the young revolutionary stirred the passions of most Bharatiyas.

REMEMBERING A HERO

On the birth centenary of Bhagat Singh, poet folklorist Ved Prakash Vatuk offers a detailed overview of the life and times of one of the most beloved heroes of India's freedom struggle. Year 2007 has been an important year for Indians. India is celebrating the 150th anniversary of the first independence war. The Indian government has sanctioned 1.5 billion rupees for the country-wide show. At the same time this is the centenary year of the birthdays of Bhagat Singh, Sukhdev and Rajguru. That too is being observed throughout India-more by the people than the government. And this is the year when India completed sixty years as an independent country. All in all, this has been a year full of patriotism.

The 150th anniversary of the first war of independence is being celebrated with much pomp and show. Hundreds of cultural shows, exhibitions, seminars and other activities are organized all over India. However, in spite of all the hoopla, all these shows remained mere junkets where participation of the public remained dismal. Many of these shows were inaugurated by the people in power, like the prime minister, governors, etc., and the audience participation in most of them was by invitation only. They were all full of patriotic slogans and very little new was learnt from them. It was an exercise in hero worshipping. No objective analysis, no lessons to be learnt.

On the other hand the martyrdom of Bhagat Singh, Sukhdev and Rajguru was fondly remembered by people all over India. These martyrs have become legends in their life time-especially Bhagat Singh. In a way the martyrdom of these heroes is the climax of the revolutionary movements which freed India. In this article we will focus on Bhagat Singh and his times.

The story of Bhagat Singh can not be told just by describing his life alone. Bhagat Singh was a symbol of sacrifice for and selfless devotion to humanity. However, his story began long before he was born. Several generations before him his ancestors were involved in a struggle against colonial rule and injustice. After the death of Maharaja Ranjit Singh in 1839, the British fought to occupy Punjab. At that time one of Bhagat Singh's ancestors, Fateh Singh, fought against them. And the same Fateh Singh participated in the first independence war, which the British writers called the great mutiny of 1857. Naturally he suffered when the British survived. He lost his property.

Fateh Singh had a son named Gurbachan Singh. One of Gurbachan Singh's three sons was Arjun Singh, the grandfather of Bhagat Singh. Arjun Singh met Swami Dayananda Saraswati, founder of the Arya Samaj, when the Swami was touring Punjab. He was so impressed by the Swami that he decided to join the Arya Samaj and dedicate his life to reform Hindu society. At the same time he got involved in the freedom movement. It was he who at the time of the yanjopaveet ceremony for his grandsons-Bhagat Singh and Jagat Singh-declared, "I give these two grandsons to be sacrificed at the altar of goddess liberty." The grandsons kept their grandfather's pledge-they would indeed dedicate their life to the freedom movement.

Arjun Singh had three sons. In 1878 his eldest son Kishan Singh, father of all his grandchildren, was born. After graduating from Anglo Sanskrit High School, Jalandhar, he became a great supporter of Mahatma Hansraj, a great devotee of Swami Dayananda Saraswati. He helped victims of famines, plagues, earthquakes and floods from 1898 to 1905 in different parts of India. He came into contact with Gadar heroes like Kartar Singh Sarabha and Rash Behari Bose and completely dedicated his life to the freedom movement. He was jailed for his activities. Thus he gave his children, Bhagat Singh among them, lessons in patriotism from the day they were born.

Kishan Singh's younger brother Ajit Singh (1881-1947) also got involved in the freedom movement after graduating from the same high school. In his college days he gave talks asking fellow students to dedicate their life to the service of the nation. He was greatly influenced by Lokmanya Bal Gangadhar Tilak. He became a close friend of Sufi Amba Prasad when the latter was released from prison after serving a five-year sentence for his involvement in the freedom movement.

They along with Ajit Singh's brothers Kishan Singh and Swarn Singh and other revolutionaries founded Bharat Mata Society. Ajit Singh was one of main leaders in the peasant movement which protested the increase of irrigation taxes and the exploitation of the peasants by moneylenders. The slogan pagree sambhaal jatta-Oh peasant, guard your turban (honor)-became the mantra of the movements.

He was jailed for his participation in this movement. Later he was exiled along with Sufi Amba Prasad and Lala Lajpat Rai. Ajit Singh could return to India only after 39 years in 1947. He died on August 15, 1947, the day India became free.

This was the legacy to which Bhagat Singh was born on September 28, 1907 in this revolutionary family in the village Kharkharkalan, District Jalandhar, the day his uncle Ajit Singh came to their village after being released from jail. Since his birth he found his home to be the center of revolutionary activities, where freedom fighters congregated and debated the ways to work for India's freedom. As described above his grandfather had decided at his yajnopaveet ceremony that he was to dedicate all his life serving the nation. There is a legend about him that when Bhagat Singh was five years old, his family was sowing sugarcane in a field. He put a rifle in place of a sugarcane piece. When asked what he was doing he answered that he was sowing rifles, so that they can be used to chase the British away from India. After graduating from high school Bhagat Singh joined the National College of Lahore, an institution founded by the famous Congress leader Lala Lajpat Rai, who was called Panjab Kesari (the Lion of Punjab) by the people. This institution did not produce clerks or civil servants for the British rule, but prepared its students to fight for freedom.

Here, besides Lalaji he came into contact with Gadar hero Bhai Parmanand, who taught history. Bhai Parmanand had already served the harsh sentence in kala pani-Andaman Nicobar's Cellular Jail-where the most dangerous prisoners were sent.

It was at this time when Mahatma Gandhi launched the first non-cooperation movement. Bhagat Singh was greatly influenced by Gandhiji. But when Gandhiji withdrew the movement because of violence in Chauri Chaura, in which many policemen were murdered, Bhagat Singh, like many young men, was disappointed. To them Gandhiji's non-violence was only a tactic and not a dharma. They decided that there was only one way to free India and that was the way of armed revolution.

As we can see, Bhagat Singh was influenced by a variety of thoughts and people. In his young age he was a staunch Arya Samaji, he was greatly influenced by the Gadar movement. Its youngest hero Kartar Singh Sarabha, who was hanged by the British at the age of 19, became his political guru. He kept Sarabha's photograph in his pocket. He was greatly moved by the heroes of Kakori Case.

Its martyrs Ram Prasad Bismil, Ashfaqullah, Rajendra Lahiri and Thakur Roshan Singh inspired him immensely. The massacre of Jallianwala Bagh left a deep impression on the mind of teenage Bhagat Singh. Later he was absorbed in the study of various European revolutions which left a deep impression on him. Bhagat Singh's mind was like a house whose windows were open on all sides and all revolutionary thoughts entered in like a free breeze. Throughout his life he kept churning these ideas logically until he became a rationalist, Marxist, atheist, revolutionary willing to sacrifice his life to kindle the flame of revolution.

It was 1928. The British government, besieged by the unrest in India, decided to send the Simon Commission to India to find out what kind of reforms would appease Indians. Since there was no Indian member in the commission and since Indians were fooled so many times by the British before, Indians decided to boycott the commission.

In every city the commission went it was met with black flags and protests. "Simon go back," became the united call. When they came to Lahore on Oct. 20, 1928, a huge protest march was led by the prominent Congress leaders Madan Mohan Malviya and Panjab Kesari Lala Lajpat Rai to oppose their arrival.

The police superintendent ordered cane charge on the peaceful crowd. Lala Lajpat Rai was attacked severely and he died because of the blows showered on him on Nov. 17. The whole country was stunned by this savage blow on the most respected leader. Lalaji's last words were, "Each blow on my head will become the nail in the British rule's casket."

Bhagat Singh and his other friends, members of the Naujawan Sabha and Hindustan Socialist Republican Army, were outraged. They had to retaliate to show that Indian youths were not dead and they would show the British they would avenge the death of their beloved elderly leader. On Dec. 17, 1928, they were ready. When a red motorcycle started from the police office, they fired.

Unfortunately, the rider was not the police superintendent but his assistant. Next day the hand bills appeared on walls all over Lahore that the death of Lalaji had been avenged and the honour of the nation was upheld. Bhagat Singh escaped and with the help of his friends-Sukhdev and Durga "Bhabhi" along with his leader Chandrashekhar Azad went to Kolkata fooling the police who were everywhere.

Instead of paying attention to their grievances, the colonial government tried to suppress Indian masses even more. In order to suppress workers, who were going on strikes to demand better treatment, the government decided to introduce the Trade Dispute Bill along with another bill to curb mass movements called the Public Safety Bill. Those bills were brought before the Central Legislative Assembly. Even when the assembly rejected them the viceroy used his veto power and declared them adopted.

The declaration of the adoption of these bills was to take place on April 8, 1929. The Hindustani Socialist Republican Army decided to protest that by throwing a bomb in the Assembly. The party took inspiration from a French anarchist Auguste Vaillant (1861-1893) who threw a bomb in the French Chambers of Deputies in 1893 in revenge of the execution of his comrade Rovachol. He shouted, "It takes a loud voice to make the deaf hear." When he was hanged for his action, he shouted "Death to the bourgeoisie. Long live anarchy." Bhagat Singh changed that slogan to, "Death to imperialism. Long live revolution." When I was a child we used to shout in the rallies, Inqalab zindabad, British hakoomat ho barbad (Long live Revolution, Down with the British Government.)

HSRA was not prepared to send Bhagat Singh to throw the bomb in the Assembly. But when Sukhdev teased him that he wanted to save his neck while pretending to be a revolutionary, Bhagat Singh became agitated and insisted to Azad that he had to do that. Finally he and Batukeshwar Dutt were selected to do the job. At the appointed time, when the bills were to be declared adopted on April 8, 1929.

Bhagat Singh and Batukeshwar Dutt threw the bomb in the empty space of the assembly, declaring: "It takes a loud voice to make the dead hear. This British Government thrust upon the helpless but unwilling Indian nation is no better than an organized gang of robbers." They declared that freedom is a birth right of everyone.

The bomb created panic. The assembly was soon empty except for two or three Indian leaders, Malviya among them. Bhagat Singh and Batukeshwar Dutt did not run away. They stood and courted arrest-like brave soldiers of war.

These two episodes made Bhagat Singh a household name, a legend in his own time. Women and men composed songs. They sang them at various occasions-at weddings, while grinding corn and working in fields. Ever since I began to talk and understand I grew up singing these songs at the lap of my brother and father-both freedom fighters.

Bhagat Singh insisted that he was not a terrorist, but a revolutionist. He said again and again that individual terrorism can never bring freedom. He loved life and he and his friends were sorry that they took the life of a British policeman as a human being, but sometimes it is unavoidable to take a life of a person representing a tyrannical repressive rule.

Bhagat Singh and his comrades used the trial as a tool to further awareness of their cause. They explained their philosophy of revolution, motives of their actions and telling their friends outside what to do. Soon the government caught up with their game and they were suddenly tried by a tribunal instead of the lower court.

Again and again Bhagat Singh emphasized that he was a revolutionary. And by revolution he meant "the ultimate establishment of an order of society which may not be threatened by such breakdown and in which the sovereignty of the proloteriat should be recognized and a world federation should redeem humanity from the bondage of capitalism and misery of imperial wars." To him this revolution was an inalienable right of mankind.

To him, like Lokmanya Tilak, freedom was an imperishable birthright of all. "Revolution means complete overthrow of the existing social order and its replacement with the socialistic order." To Bhagat Singh freedom did not mean merely replacing the white faces with black ones on the throne. Like the Gadar heroes, Bhagat Singh also wanted a casteless, classless, society free from all kinds of social and economic exploitation.

Unfortunately we pay homange to the image of Bhagat Singh who holds a pistol in his hand, not that of a true revolutionary. We don't admire him for his great love for literature, his fondness of poetry. During the time he spent in his jail cell before he was hanged, he read continuously. His study did not stop at revolutionary books or Marxist literature. He read novels by many American authors of his time. His jail notebook is full of quotations from all genres of literature and subjects-love, marriage, revolution, you name it. He must have read close to two hundred books.

Today the tragedy is that everyone wants to cash in on the martyrdom of Bhagat Singh. Even those religious institutions who did not give a damn about the Gadari babas or Bhagat Singh today want to arrange akhand path in their memory.

To me it is an insult to Bhagat Singh-a rationalist, atheist-to place his portrait next to fundamentalish Sikh separatist Jarnail Singh Bhindranwale. To me at is an insult to Bhagat Singh when the Haryana chief minister proposes to build a statue in his honour, because he was a "true Arya Samaji."

To me it is also an insult to Bhagat Singh when the armchair leftist historians want to use him to condemn Gandhiji. They blame Bhagat Singh's execution on Gandhiji.

On this score let us be clear. Did Bhagat Singh want to live? He is his own best witness for that. Like Kartar Singh Sarabha, Ram Prasad Bismil, Thakur Roshan Singh and Ashfaqullah, Bhagat Singh, too, felt that his martyrdom will serve their country better.

Bhagat Singh was so angry when his own father tried to save his life and sent a petition to the government that he rebuked his father in no uncertain terms.

He felt sorry that his father showed weakness. He told his father that he had put no defense for himself at the trial and he did not want to live devoid of his principles. "My life is not at all worth living at the cost of my principles" Anyone who can rebuke his father in such a harsh way could have never wished anybody including Gandhiji to beg for mercy on his behalf, especially when Bhagat Singh and Sukhdev in several communications rejected Gandhi's way of thoughts.

Let me quote extensively from Bhagat Singh's statement. "I make no secret of the fact that it is but natural for me to desire to remain alive. But I can live only under certain conditions. I refuse to live in prison or parole. My name has become the focal point of the party of revolution and its sacrifices have placed me on an elevated pedestal. This pedestal is so high that if I survive by being spared I will not be able to live up to that standard. My weaknesses are not generally known and the public is unaware of them. If I manage to cheat the gallows, they will be exposed for all to see. Maybe the revolutionary fire in me will cool down. it may be even extinguished."

He further writes:

"But if I am hanged like a brave man, with a smile on my face, Indian mothers will encourage their children to emulate my example. Our hangings will substantially add to the number of martyrs in the cause of the freedom of our motherland, so much that it will be impossible any longer for the satanic powers of imperialism to resist the Revolution."

On November 30, 1930 Bhagat Singh wrote to Batukeshwar Dutt:

"(I) am anxiously waiting for the day when I will be fortunate enough to embrace the gallows for my ideals. I will climb the gallows gladly and show the world how bravely the revolutionaries can sacrifice themselves to the cause."

Bhagat Singh is a hero because of his martyrdom. When I look at the life of those heroes, who were no less heroic or deep thinkers than Bhagat Singh, but who survived gallows, I feel sad. Shiv Varma, Durga Bhabhi, Batukeshwar Dutt and many others were not remembered by the masses even when they died. How many people know about the youngest prisoner of Kakori case, who served fourteen years in prison? His name-famous Hindi novelist Manmathnath Gupta.

With all due respect to my armchair leftist historian friends, I would like to close the article by quoting Gandhi. In Gandhi's tribute to these heroes, who were hanged at 7 pm on March 23, I feel the whole nation paid tribute to them.

Gandhi wrote in Young India March 29, 1931 issue:

"Bhagat Singh and his two associates have been hanged. The Congress made many attempts to save their lives and the government entertained many hopes of it, but all has been in a vain.

"Bhagat Singh did not wish to live. He refused to apologize or even file an appeal. Bhagat Singh was not a devotee of non-violence, but he did not subscribe to the religion of violence. He took to violence due to helplessness and to defend his homeland. In his last letter Bhagat Singh wrote: 'I have been arrested while waging a war. For me there are no gallows. Put me into the mouth of a cannon and blow me off.'

"These heroes have conquered the fear of death. Let us bow to them a thousand times for their heroism."

BHAGAT SINGH AND ATHEISM

Bhagat Singh was not only one of India's greatest freedom fighters and revolutionary socialists, but also one of its early Marxist thinkers and ideologues. Unfortunately, this last aspect is relatively unknown with the result that all sorts of reactionaries, obscurantist and communalists have been wrongly and dishonestly trying to utilize for their own politics and ideologies the name of Bhagat Singh and his comrades such as Chandra Shekhar Azad.

Bhagat Singh died young at the age of 23. His political thought and practice started evolving very early when he made a quick transition from Gandhian nationalism to revolutionary terrorism. But already by 1927-28 he began to move from revolutionary terrorism to Marxism. During the years 1925 to 1928, Bhagat Singh read voraciously, devouring in particular books on the Russian Revolution and the Soviet Union, even though getting hold of such books was in itself at the time a revolutionary and difficult task. In the 1920s, Bhagat Singh was one of the most well-read persons in India on revolutionary movements, anarchism and Marxism.

He also tried to inculcate the reading and thinking habit among his fellow revolutionaries and younger comrades. He asserted during his trial before the Lahore High Court that "the sword of revolution is sharpened at the whetstone of thought".

Already by the end of 1928, he and his comrades had accepted socialism as the final object of their activities and changed the name of their organization from the Hindustan Republican Association to Hindustan Socialist Republican Association.

From now on, before his arrest in June 1929 and after, Bhagat Singh's furious march towards the acquisition and mastery of Marxism continued unabated. In the process, he brought under critical scrutiny all contemporary views, including his own, regarding the nationalist movement, the character of the contemporary worldwide revolutionary process, anarchism, socialism, violence and nonviolence, revolutionary terrorism, religion, communalism, older revolutionaries and contemporary nationalists, etc.

It is one of the greatest tragedies of our people that this giant of a brain was brought to a stop so early by the colonial authorities. In this small pamphlet* are brought before the reader two relatively unknown articles written by Bhagat Singh in jail during 1930-31, while he was awaiting the action of the gallows. In these articles, as in numerous other letters, statements and articles, he clearly emerges as a revolutionary fully committed to Marxism and capable of applying it with the full complexity of its method.

In the first article, Bhagat Singh deals with religion and atheism. He traces his own path to atheism though influenced in early childhood by religion and later by the early revolutionary terrorists such as Sachindra Nath Sanyal, whose book Bandi Jivan was a basic textbook for all revolutionaries during the 1920s. These early revolutionaries relied upon religion and mysticism to acquire the spiritual strength they revealed in their immensely courageous activities. In this article, as also in the second, Bhagat Singh shows full understanding of the approach and viewpoint of the early revolutionaries and traces the source of their religiosity. He points out that in the absence of a scientific understanding of their own political activity, they needed irrational religious beliefs and mysticism to sustain themselves spiritually, to struggle against personal temptation, to overcome depression, to be able to sacrifice their physical comforts, families and even life.

When one is constantly willing to risk one's life and make all other sacrifices, a person requires deep sources of inspiration. This necessary need was, in the case of early revolutionary terrorists, met by mysticism and religion.

But these were no longer necessary as sources of inspiration for those who understood the nature of their activity, who had advanced to a revolutionary ideology, who could struggle against oppression without artificial spiritual crutches, who could confidently and without fear mount the gallows without requiring the consolation and comfort of `eternal' salvation, who fought for freedom and emancipation of the oppressed because they "could not do otherwise".

Bhagat Singh was himself at the time waiting for the noose to fall around his neck. He knew that at such a moment it was easy to take recourse to God. "In God man can W d very strong consolation and support".

On the other hand, to depend on one's own inner strength was not easy. As he put it: "To stand upon one's own legs amid storms and hurricanes is not a child's play". He also knew that the task required immense moral strength and that the modern revolutionaries were following a moral path of a unique nature. This path led one to devote oneself to " the service of mankind and emancipation of the suffering humanity".

This was the path followed by men and women who dared "to challenge the oppressors, exploiters, and tyrants" and who, opposing "mental stagnation", insisted on thinking for themselves. As Bhagat Singh further put it: "Criticism and independent thinking are the two indispensable qualities of a revolutionary". Bhagat Singh points out that it is not easy to live the life of a reasoning person. It is easy to take consolation or relief from blind faith. But it is our duty to try ceaselessly to live the life of reason. And that is why Bhagat Singh asserts at the end of the essay that by proclaiming himself an atheist and a realist (materialist) he was "trying to stand like a man with an erect head to the last; even on the gallows".

In Bhagat Singh's analysis of religion and its basic causation, we get a glimpse of his powerful intellect, his revolutionary commitment and his capacity to think in a historical, materialist and scientific manner.

Religion, he notes, is not merely created by the ruling and exploiting classes to deceive the people, to legitimize their class privileges and power, and to keep the people socially quiet, though it also serves that purpose in real life and therefore it becomes an ally and instrument of these classes. But religion is much more the consequence of the inability of the primitive man to fully understand his natural environment, to understand his own social activity and social organization, and to control his own life and overcome its limitations. God then becomes a useful myth. This myth was "useful to the society in the primitive age".

Moreover, "the idea of God is helpful to man in distress". God and religion enabled the helpless individual to face life with courage. "God was brought into imaginary existence to encourage man to face boldly all the trying circumstances, to meet all dangers manfully and to check and restrain his outbursts in prosperity and affluence". "Belief softens the hardships, even can make them pleasant. In God man can find very strong consolation and support". Thus, to the distressed, the betrayed and the helpless, God serves as "a father mother, sister and brother, friend and helper" 2

But, says Bhagat Singh, when science has grown and when the oppressed begin to struggle for their self-emancipation, when " man tries to stand on his own legs and become a realist (Bhagat Singh uses this word in place of rationalist and materialist)", the need for God , this artificial crutch, this imaginary saviour comes to an end. In this struggle for self-emancipation, it becomes necessary to fight against "the narrow conception of religion" as also against the belief in God. "Any man who stands for progress", says Bhagat Singh, "has to criticise, disbelieve and challenge every item of the old faith. Item by item he has to reason out every nook and corner of the prevailing faith.... A man who claims to be a realist has to challenge the whole of the ancient faith.... the first thing for him is to shatter the whole down and clear a space for the erection of a new philosophy".

Bhagat Singh's sympathetic though critical understanding of his predecessors, his capacity to place philosophic and political approaches and ideas in a historical setting, and his basic Marxist reasoning also emerge clearly in his discussion of several other issues.

In the second essay, An Introduction to The Dreamland, the poetical work of the old revolutionary Lala Ram Saran Das, sentenced to transportation for life in 1915, Bhagat Singh indirectly traces the change from the earlier `pure' nationalism, based on the single idea of overthrowing foreign domination, to a nationalism that was simultaneously committed to the total reconstitution of the existing social order. Writing more like a poet than a political-philosophical commentator, Bhagat Singh first establishes his own generation's continuity with the old revolutionaries from whom it imbibed the spirit of nationalism, love of the people and the capacity to sacrifice. He then brings out his philosophical, political and ideological differences with them.

In the very beginning of the essay, he brings out, as already discussed in an earlier section of this introduction, the difference between their reliance on mysticism and religiosity for inspiration and his own firm commitment to materialism, reason and science.

He also deals with the contemporary and complex and vexed question of violence and nonviolence. Going to the heart of the matter, he describes how the revolutionaries want to build a social order from which violence in all its forms will be eliminated, in which reason and justice will prevail and all questions will be settled by argument and education. But this is precisely what imperialists, capitalists and other exploiters will not permit. Instead, they mercilessly suppress any effort to evolve socialism through education of the people and by peaceful methods. Hence, revolutionaries have to adopt violence as " a necessary item of their programme". The entire question is brilliantly summed up when Bhagat Singh says that the revolutionaries "have to resort to violent means as a terrible necessity". Once socialist power is established, methods of education and persuasion would be employed to develop society; force would be used only to remove the obstacles.

In his essay on Atheism also he had put the issue in the same way. The new generation of revolutionaries had replaced "the Romance of the violent methods alone which was so prominent amongst our predecessors", and had come to believe that the "use of force (was) justifiable when resorted to as a matter of terrible necessity", while "nonviolence as policy (was) indispensable for all mass movements". Thus the revolutionaries do not glorify violence; revolution is not based on the cult of violence. At the same time, revolutionaries do not shun the necessary violence. Where history and the ruling classes force upon them, they take recourse to it as a "terrible necessity" in order to overthrow the existing social order.

Bhagat Singh simultaneously sees the utopian character of much of early revolutionary thinking, the positive historic role that utopians play in certain stages of social movements and social development, and the inevitable decline of utopias once the revolutionary movement starts acquiring a scientific outlook and philosophy on the basis of "scientific Marxian Socialism":

Bhagat Singh deals at length with one aspect of utopian thought: How to combine mental and physical labour? He accepts that elimination of the gap between the two is basic to the building of a socialist society. But this elimination, he feels, cannot be brought about by mechanical and utopian means suggested by Ram Saran Das such as making all mental workers do physical and mental labour for 4 hours a day: The nature of physical and mental labour is different.

The root of the problem lies in the existing inequality between the two. The answer lies in treating both as productive labour and opposing the notion that mental workers are superior to manual workers. Lastly, Bhagat Singh was a critical revolutionary in the best traditions of Marx, Engels and Lenin. Asking young men to read The Dreamland, he warns: "Do not read it to follow blindly and take for granted what is written in it. Read it, criticise it, think over it, and try to formulate your own ideas with its help".

THE TRIBUNAL

The Lahore Conspiracy Case ordinance, under which the Tribunal was established, was promulgated by the Governor-General Lord Irwin allegedly in exercise of the power conferred by S.72 of the Government of India Act, 1919. The said Act, however, stipulated that the Governor-General's Ordinance could not have a life of more than six months and that it could only be made in "cases of emergency".

There was no such emergency. But, in the light of the tremendous and growing popularity of Bhagat Singh and his comrades and the infectious example which they set for others, the colonial authorities were determined on a course of reckless haste and securing a shortcut to the gallows, especially for Bhagat Singh. There was to be no jury and no appeal against the Tribunal's decision, whose members were removable at will-as indeed two of them were within two months of its being constituted. If the accused were too weak to attend (as for instance consequent upon hunger strike) or would not attend as a political protest against unreasonable police or court behaviour, the trial could proceed in absentia.

This was no judicial tribunal. It was a political court, blatantly used as a political weapon by the autocratic alien authorities to snuff out the finest sons of India-in defiance of all norms of justice and fairness.

The Tribunal began its proceedings on 5 May 1930. After the accused were badly treated and handled roughly in the court on 12 May, they participated no further in the proceedings, which were 'continued' in their absence. The requests of the defence for cross examining all the prosecution witnesses and for more time to enable the defence to go through the evidence were rejected by the Tribunal-all in the rush to conclude the case before the 6-month period after which the appointment of the Tribunal would lapse, and with it the Tribunal itself, thus invalidating the entire proceedings. So the prosecutor abruptly closed his case before the Tribunal on 26 August so as to bring it to completion before the 31 October 1930 deadline. On 10 September, Carden Noad finished his concluding speech. Less than a month later, on 7 October 1930, the Special Tribunal to try the Lahore Conspiracy Case delivered its judgement, acquitting three and convicting all others. While Bhagat Singh, Sukhdev and Rajguru were sentenced to death, seven were transported for life, the remaining two were given rigorous imprisonment terms of seven and five years.

Even Nehru, whose attitude, for reasons of class and self interest, as well as the malign influence of Gandhi's one-sided nonviolence, with its insistence of nonviolence by the masses in the face of the brutality of the exploiting classes, was always marked by ambivalence, reacted to the Court's verdict with considerable anger and aguish. In a speech at Allahabad on 12 October 1930, he said: "If England were invaded by Germany..., would Lord Irwin go about advising the people to refrain from violence against the invader? If he is not prepared to do that, let him not raise the issue. It is for Mahatma Gandhi and others, who believe with him, to do so.... But let there be no mistake about it. Whether I agree with him or not, my heart is full of admiration for the courage and self-sacrifice of a man like Bhagat Singh. Courage of the Bhagat Singh type is exceedingly rare. If the Viceroy expects us to refrain from admiring this wonderful courage and the high purpose behind it, he is mistaken. Let him ask his own heart what he would have felt if Bhagat Singh had been an Englishman and acted for England."

IMPACT OF LENIN

Bhagat Singh was born in Punjab on September 28, 1907, and was hanged by the British on March 23, 1931. So it may be said that in his short life-span of 24 years political activities covered at the most a period of seven to eight years. The young Indian revolutionary was sentenced to death before he could reach his thirties. It should not be expected that his concepts regarding revolution were full-fledged and mature and had taken definite shape at such an early age. Yet, his short political career which came to an abrupt end gave remarkable and significant colour to his thought and actions.

Bhagat Singh did not come from a mere nationalist background. His family had a distinct revolutionary heritage. His father, Sardar Kishan Singh, and his uncles, Sardar Ajit Singh and Sardar Swaran Singh, were all connected with the Bharat Mata Samiti, the oldest revolutionary organisation in Punjab. They had to suffer greatly at the hands of the British. Ajit Singh, who was initially exiled to Burma in 1907, had to escape from his motherland to Iran, Turkey, Germany, and ultimately to Brazil.

Coming as he did from such a family, in his childhood and adolescent years Bhagat Singh naturally came in close contact with well-known revolutionaries like Lala Pindi Das, Ananda Kishore Mehta and others. To young Bhagat Singh, Kartar Singh Sarava, the Ghadr Party leader, was like a mythical hero. In 1916 young Sarava had become a martyr at an even younger age than Bhagat Singh. So in his formative years his family and environment had left a deep nationalist and revolutionary impact on Bhagat Singh. While studying in the National College he had met Professor Jaychandra Vidyalankar and students like Bhagwaticharan, Sukhdev, Yashpal and Ramkishen who later earned fame as prominent revolutionaries.

Bhagat Singh went to Kanpur in 1924 and was introduced to Batukeshwar Dutta, Bejoy Kumar Sinha, Jogesh Chattopadhyay and other revolutionaries of the region by Ganesh Shankar Vidyarthi, the famous Congress leader of UP. (It may be mentioned that this is also the 50th year of Ganesh Shankar Vidyarthi's martyrdom. He died while participating in the anti-comunal movement.) Bhagat Singh became a member of the group known as the Hindustan Republican Association (HRA) because of his intimate ties with these revolutionaries.

In the constitution of the revolutionary group it was declared that the ultimate aim of the organisation was to establish a federal republican form of government in India through organised and armed revolution.....The fundamental principles of this Republic would be establishing universal suffrage and eradicating the social system in which there is class-exploitation.

The programme of the HRA also spoke of 'organising workers and peasants'. In spite of the close watch by the imperialist guardians of India, some news of the remarkable success of Soviet society and communism reached India. It seems all these revolutionaries were greatly influenced by those developments.

BHAGAT SINGH'S LAST DAYS

Meanwhile, as the judgment day neared, unable to contain his paternal feelings, Bhagat Singh's father, Kishen Singh, petitioned the Tribunal in a last desperate effort to save his son's life. On hearing of his father's petition, Bhagat Singh was incandescent with rage and wrote to his father a remonstrative letter, which brings out clearly Bhagat Singh's exacting standards of conduct-standards which he followed and expected others, including those he dearly loved and respected, to abide by. Bhagat Singh's letter, published in full by The Tribune on 4 October, just three days before the Tribunal's judgement, reflects not only his legendary courage, fidelity to principle and indomitable spirit of self-sacrifice, but also the deeply-felt injury to his feelings inflicted on him by the father that he loved and respected. This is what, inter alia, Bhagat Singh wrote to his father on this occasion:

"My dear father,

"I was astounded to learn that you had submitted a petition to the members of the Special Tribunal in connection with my defence. This intelligence proved to be too severe a blow to be borne with equanimity. It has upset the whole equilibrium of my mind. I have not been able to understand how you could think it proper to submit such a petition at this stage and in these circumstances. In spite of all the sentiments and feelings of a father, I don't think you were at all entitled to make such a move on my behalf without even consulting me.

"My life is not so precious, at least to me, as you may probably think it to be. It is not at all worth buying at the cost of my principles. There are other comrades of mine whose case is as serious as that of mine. We had adopted a common policy and we shall stand to the last, no matter how dearly we have to pay individually for it.

"Father, I am quite perplexed. I fear I might overlook the ordinary principle of etiquette and my language may become a little but harsh while criticising or censoring this move on your part. Let me be candid. I feel as though I have been stabbed in the back. Had any other person done it, I would have considered it to be nothing short of treachery. But in your case, let me say that it has been a weakness-a weakness of the worst type.

"This was the time when everybody's mettle was being tested. Let me say, father, you have failed. I know you are as sincere a patriot as one can be. I know you have devoted your life to the cause of Indian independence, but why, at this moment, have you displayed such a weakness? I cannot understand.

"In the end, I would like to inform you and my other friends and all the people interested in my case that I have not approved of your move.

"I want that the public should know all the details about this complication, and therefore, I request you to publish this letter.

"Your loving son, Bhagat Singh"

On 3 March 1931, Bhagat Singh saw his family for the last time. Distressed by the tearful sight of his younger brother Kultar in tears, Bhagat Singh wrote to him a letter-at once moving and inspiring. The original, written in Urdu, is reproduced here in Roman alphabet with a translation. The reason for this is that as the English translation does not do justice to the powerful verses that Bhagat quoted in the original, those of our readers who have some knowledge of the Urdu language might thus be enabled to gauge in full the depth of ideas and powerful emotions expressed by Bhagat Singh in his very concise letter.

"3 March 1931

"Aziz Kultar,

"Aaj tumhari aankhon mein aansu dekh kar bahut ranj hua. Aaj tumhari baat mein bahut dard tha. Tumhare aansu mujh se bardasht nahin huye.

"Barkhurdar, himmat se taalim hasil karte jana aur sehat ka khayal rakhna.

"Hausla rakhna. Aur kya... (likhun?)... Shaer main kya kahun suno:

Usay yeh fikr hardam naya tarze jafa kya hai,

Hamen yeh shauq hai dekhen sitam ki intiha kya hai.

Dair se kyun khafa rahen aur kyun gila Karen,

Hamara jahan hai sahi, ao muqabla Karen.

Koi dam ka mehman hoon ai ahle mehfil,

Chiraghe sahar hoon, bujha chahta hoon.

Mere hawa mein rahegi khayal ki khushboo,

Yeh mushte khaq hai, fani rahe na rahe.

"Achha rukhsat.

Khush raho ahle watan hum to safar karte hain.

"Hausle se rehna

"Namaste.

"Tumhara Bhai, Bhagat Singh"

English translation of the original letter:

"3 March 1931

"Dear Kultar,

"It made me very sad to see tears in your eyes today. There was deep pain in your words today. I could not bear to see your tears.

"My boy, pursue your studies with determination and look after your health.

"Be determined. What else... (can I write?)... What couplets can I recite? Listen:

They are ever anxious to devise new forms of treachery,

We are eager to see what limits there are to oppression.

Why should we be angry with the world... and complain,

Ours is a just world (ideal), let us fight for it.

I am a guest only for a few moments, my companions,

I am the lamp that burns before the dawn and longs to be extinguished.

The breeze will spread the essence of my thoughts,

This self is but a fistful of dust, whether it lives or perishes.

"Well, goodbye.

Be happy, countrymen, I am off to travel.

"Live courageously.

"Namaste.

"Your brother, Bhagat Singh".

Whereas the first eight lines are from a poem by Mohamed Iqbal, one of the greatest poets of the Indian sub-continent, the last line, appearing just after the words, "well, goodbye", is from Wajid Ali Shah, which the latter recited when the British East India Company evicted him from Lucknow after deposing him from the throne and the annexation of Oudh. The original reads thus:

"Dar-o-deewar pe hasrat se nazar karte hain

Kush raho ahle watan hum to safar karte hain".

"I cast my eyes longingly at the doors and the walls

Be happy, countrymen, I am off to travel."

Bhagat Singh deliberately omitted the first line of the above couplet. A.G. Nourani, the author of the excellent book, The Trial of Bhagat Singh, makes the correct observation that this studious omission "... speaks a lot for Bhagat Singh's refinement of feeling as well as courage", for "Bhagat Singh felt no longing for the world from which he was about to depart. He did not care to cast his eyes back. He left the world cheerfully fortified in the knowledge that he would live as a symbol of integrity and courage in the hearts and minds of his countrymen" (pp. 231-232).

As the end of life approached nearer and nearer, Bhagat Singh's firm belief in a socialist and communist future became ever more ardent. Just a few days prior to his judicial murder, in his March 1931 letter to the Governor of Punjab, he expressed himself thus: "Let us declare that the state of war does exist and shall exist so long as the Indian toiling masses and their natural resources are being exploited by a handful of parasites.

They may be purely British capitalists, or mixed British and Indian, or even purely Indian. They may be carrying on their insidious exploitation through mixed or even purely Indian bureaucratic apparatus. All these things make no difference.... This war shall continue.... It shall be waged with new vigour, greater audacity and unflinching determination till the socialist republic is established".

At a time when all seems to have been lost, to have written the above lines showed a remarkable degree of knowledge and understanding of the laws of history, not to speak of the determination and cheerful optimism and audacity that is expressed in them At a time when the alien rulers of India were universally hated by the Indian masses, to have expressed the idea that the struggle to overthrow the system of exploitation would continue its relentless march even if the place of the British exploiters was taken by Indian exploiters, was remarkable for its time in India and revealed an ability to see well beyond the struggle for freedom from alien subjugation and oppression.

Alluding to the unrivalled sacrifices of Jatin Das, Bhagwati Charan Vohra and Chandrashekar Azad, Bhagat Singh concluded his letter by telling the Punjab Governor that, since the court in its verdict had emphasised that he and his fellow revolutionaries had waged war against the British Crown, they were prisoners of war and, therefore, entitled to "... claim to be shot instead of being hanged". Bhagat Singh went on to say that it "... rests with you [the Governor] to prove that you seriously meant what your court has said and prove it through action. We very earnestly request you and hope that you will very kindly order the Military Department to send a detachment or a shooting party to perform our execution" (A.G. Nourani, p.227).

To the very end of his life Bhagat Singh remained thoughtful and incisive in the extreme. On 22 March, one day before he was hanged, his fellow revolutionaries in jail sent him a note in which they asked the question if he would desire to live.

His answer, as ever sagacious, portrays the following picture of the relation between his desire to live and the purpose of that life, as well as the relation between the sacrifices of the revolutionary party and the heights to which he had been elevated: "The desire to live is natural.

It is in me also. I do not want to conceal it. But it is conditional. I don't want to live as a prisoner or under restrictions. My name has become a symbol of the Indian revolution. The ideals and the sacrifices of the revolutionary party have elevated me to a height beyond which I will never be able to rise if I live...

Yes, one thing pricks me even today. My heart nurtured some ambitions for doing something for humanity and for my country. I have not been able to fulfil even one thousandth part of those ambitions.

If I live I might perhaps get a chance to fulfil them. If ever it came to my mind that I should not die, it came from this end only. I am proud of myself these days and I am anxiously waiting for the final test. I wish the day may come nearer soon. Your comrade, Bhagat Singh"

Just as in questions of politics, so in questions of religion-Bhagat Singh's fidelity to his principles and system of beliefs did not desert him even in the face of immediate death. Manmathnath Gupta, convicted in the Kakori case, has reconstructed the events of 23 March 1931, the last day in the lives of Bhagat Singh, Rajguru and Sukhdev.

On receiving the order that the hanging was to take place the same evening, the chief warder of the jail, a god-fearing man by the name of Chatar Singh, approached Bhagat Singh with a scripture and pleaded with him to pray.

Polite as ever, Bhagat Singh declined the request, saying that he had been an atheist all his life and had no wish to depart from that stance on the last day of his life. Instead, he spent the entire day reading a biography of V.I.Lenin that had been sent to him at his request. At about seven in the evening, an official of the jail came over to accompany him to the gallows.

Bhagat Singh, engrossed in the biography, said: "wait a minute, one revolutionary is busy meeting another". After reading a few more pages, he got up to undertake the final journey of his life. With the shouts of 'Long live revolution!' and 'Down with imperialism!', the three great revolutionaries-Bhagat Singh, Rajguru and Sukhdev-faced the hangman's noose.

They were hanged while singing the following lines, which have since been repeated by the masses of Indian people and which have become a symbol of the revolutionary immortality of Bhagat Singh and his comrades:

"Dil se niklegi na marker bhi watan ki ulfat,

Meri mitti se bhi khushbue watan aaegi".

"Love for the motherland will not leave my heart even after death,

Its fragrance will still be there in my dusty remains."

Rightly fearing public anger and outpouring of grief over the murder of three of the finest sons of India and apprehending public disorder over this outrage, the colonial authorities, instead of handing over the bodies to the families of these revolutionaries, in great secrecy and with indecent haste, cremated them near Ferozepur on the banks of the river Sutlej.

The reaction of the Indian people following the news of the hanging was predictable. The whole country went into mourning. Towns and villages across the vast territory of the sub-continent witnessed condolence gatherings and demonstrations. Even those who earlier had stood aside, participated in these manifestations of anger and grief.

At several places, angry crowds clashed with the police, braving firing and baton charges, which claimed more than one hundred lives. Hundreds of schools and colleges closed as a mark of respect for the departed heroes, while hundreds of thousands observed fast.

On 24 March, the day following the execution of Bhagat Singh and his comrades, in a carefully drafted statement to the press in New Delhi, Nehru stated: "I have remained absolutely silent during their last days, lest a word of mine may injure their prospect of commutation. I have remained silent, though I felt like bursting and now all is over.

"Not all of us could save him, who was so dear to us and whose magnificent courage and sacrifice have been an inspiration to the youth of India. India cannot even save her clearly loved children from the gallows.

"There will be hartals and mournings, processions everywhere. There will be sorrow in the land at our utter helplessness but there will also be pride in him who is no more, and when England speaks to us and talks of settlement there will be the corpse of Bhagat Singh between us lest we forget" (A. G. Noorani, pp. 228-229)

Nehru was doubly wrong. His silence had been unhelpful; silence, especially in the councils of the Congress Party. And, at no time in the talks between England and the Congress was the corpse of Bhagat Singh allowed to get in the way. After Indian independence and the departure of the British from India, the Indian ruling classes and the Congress Party have done their best to turn Bhagat Singh into a non-entity, a figure of peripheral significance in the Indian liberation struggle. They have failed in this mean attempt. The credit for keeping the memory of Bhagat Singh and his comrades, of keeping alive their revolutionary tradition belongs solely to the broad masses of the Indian people and the communist movement of that country.

All the same, under the pressure of the flood of sympathy, admiration and adoration for Bhagat Singh and his co-accused during their trial, and the mass outpouring of grief and volcanic eruption of popular anger following the execution of the three of them, even the leaders of the Congress Party felt obliged to swim with the tide and heap praises on Bhagat Singh. They could hardly do otherwise in view of the fact that, at that time, Bhagat Singh enjoyed far greater popularity, prestige and respect among the Indian masses than Gandhi, whose reputation lay in ruins in view of his complicity in the execution of Bhagat Singh and his comrades (of this more anon). Patibhi Sitaramyya, the historian of the Congress Party, testifies to Bhagat Singh's popularity with this understatement: "It is no exaggeration to say that at that moment Bhagat Singh's name was as widely known all over India and was as [nay, much more] popular as Gandhi's" (A. G. Noorani)

Nehru, albeit in his characteristic contradictory and confused style, emanating from a mixture of admiration and disapproval at the same time for Bhagat Singh, portrays the following picture of Bhagat Singh's popularity: "Bhagat Singh did not become popular because of his act of terrorism [Nehru is not alone in characterising all violence as terrorism-even some would-be communists are guilty of that], but because he seemed [only seemed?] to vindicate, for the moment, the honour of Lala Lajpat Rai, and through him of the nation.

He became a symbol; the act was forgotten [was it really?], the symbol [symbol unrelated to the act?] remained, and within a few months each town and village of the Punjab and to a lesser extent in the rest of northern India [nay, the whole of India], resounded with his name. Innumerable songs grew up about him, and the popularity that the man achieved was something amazing" (A. G. Noorani p.3)

A.G Noorani must have had the likes of Nehru in mind when he concluded his book with the observation: "On his [Bhagat Singh's] death, Indian leaders vied with one another in lavishing praise on him. One wonders how many of them knew then that they had lost in him a man who, had he lived, might have had an incalculable impact on the course of India's politics". Gandhi was certainly an exception to this, for he knew full well that Bhagat Singh, had he but lived, was destined to have an incalculable impact on the course of India's political development-in a direction diametrically the opposite of that desired and accomplished by the Congress under Gandhi's leadership. It was precisely for this reason that Gandhi (except once under extreme popular pressure) never lavished any praise on Bhagat Singh and played the role of an accomplice to the colonial authorities' successful efforts in sending him and his comrades to the gallows.

Four years after his execution, Bhagat Singh received a tribute from a most unlikely but most authoritative source-the Director of the Intelligence Bureau, Sir Horace Williamson. In his study India and Communism, he wrote: "Bhagat Singh made no mistake.

The prisoners' dock became a political forum and the countryside rang with his heroics. His photograph was on sale in every city and township and for a time rivalled in popularity even that of Mr Gandhi himself" (Editions Indian, Calcutta, p.275, cited by A G Noorani).

Bibliography

Alam, Kousar J. : *Political Aspects of National Integration*, Meerut: Meenakshi Prakashan, 1981.

Alva, Joachim: *Leaders of India,* Bombay, Thacker & Co., Ltd., 1943

Arabinda Poddar : *Bhagat Singh : The Political Personality*, Kolkata, Indiana, 2004.

Atri, Ajit : *Gandhi's View of Legal Justice*, New Delhi, Deep and Deep Pub., 2007.

Bose, N. K.: *The Scheduled Castes and Tribes and Their Present Conditions*, Calcutta, University of Calcutta, 1969.

Brierly, L.: *The Law of Nations,* New York, Oxford University Press, 1955.

Butalia, Urvashi: *The Other Side of Silence: Voices from the Partition of India*, New Delhi, Penguin, 1998.

Campbell-Johnson, Alan: *Mission with Bhagat Singh*, London: Hale, 1982.

Chandra, Ramesh : *History of the Freedom Movement in India*, Calcutta 1962.

Chatterji, Joya: *Bengal Divided: Hindu Communalism and Partition, 1932-1947*, Cambridge, Cambridge UP, 1994.

Chaudhuri, Nirad: *Thy Hand, Great Anarch! India: 1921-1952*, London, Chatto & Windus, 1987.

Dasai, M. H.: *Day to Day with Gandhi*, Varanasi, Sarva Sangh Pakistan, 1968.

Derrett, J. : *Religion, Law, and the State in India*, London, Faber, 1968.

Deutsch, Karl: *Political Community and the North Atlantic Area*, Princeton: Princeton University Press, 1957.

Fisher, Michael H.: *The Politics of British Annexation of India - 1757-1857,* Oxford, 1996.

Friedrich, J.: *Constitutional Government and Democracy,* Boston, Ginn, 1950.

Galanter, Marc.: *Competing Inequalities: Law and the Backward Classes in India,* University of California Press, CA, 1984.

Ghoshal, U. N.: A *History of Indian Political Ideas*. London, 1966.

Gorringe, H.: *Untouchable Citizens : Dalit Movements and Democratization in Tamil Nadu*, Delhi, Sage Publications, 2005.

Greer P.: *Transforming Central Government: the Next Steps Initiative*, Buckingham, Open University Press, 1994.

Haas, Ernst B.: *Beyond the Nation State*, Stanford: Stanford University Press, 1964.

Hasan, Mushirul: *India's Partition: Process, Strategy and Mobilization*, New Delhi, Oxford UP, 1993.

Heimanson, Rudolph: *Dictionary of Political Science and Law*, N.Y.: Oceana Publications, 1967.

Heinsath, Charles: *Indian Nationalism and Hindu Social Reform*, Princeton University Press, Princeton, 1964.

Joshi, V.C.: *Bhagat Singh and the Process of Modernization in India*, Delhi, 1975.

Kaushik, Asha : *Globalization, Democracy and Culture : Situating Gandhian Alternatives,* Jaipur, Pointer, 2002.

Krishna, B. : *Indian Freedom Struggle : The Pathfinders From Surendranath Banerjea to Gandhi*, New Delhi, Manohar, 2002.

Maheshwari, S.R.: *Public Administration in India*. The Higher Civil Service, Delhi: Oxford University Press, 2005.

Menon, Ritu and Bhasin, Kamla: *Borders and Boundaries: Women in India's Partition*, New Delhi, Kali for Women, 1998.

Menon, V. P.: *The Transfer of Power in India*, Bombay, Orient Longman, 1957.

Mosher, Frederick C.: *Democracy and the Public Service*, New York: Oxford University Press, 1968.

Nag, Sajal: *Nationalism, Separatism and Secessionism*, New Delhi: Rawat Publications, 1999.

Peddleton, E.: *Public Administration and the Public Interest,* New York, McGraw-Hill, 1936.

Singh, Balwant: *An Untouchable in the I.A.S.*, Saharanpur: Prem Printing Press, 1964.

Stanley A. Wolpert: *Bhagat Singh and Patel: Revolution and Reform in the Making of Modern India,* Berkeley, 1962.

Tarachand, S. : *History of the Freedom Movement in India,* New Delhi, 1972.

Wolpert, Stanley : *Gandhi's Passion : The Life and Legacy of Mahatma Gandhi*, Delhi, Oxford University Press, 2001.

Zaidi, A. Moin: *Evolution of Muslim political Thought in India,* New Delhi: S. Chand, 1975-79.

Index

❑❑❑